SQUARES - LINES & MORE

ADULT COLORING BOOK VOL.1

ISBN-13: 978-1523962433

ISBN-10: 1523962437

About The Artist

I grew up in an artistic family and have been an artist ever since I was a little girl.

At 17 years old I had my first professional art gallery exhibit. Later, I studied Architecture and Interior design, with my specialty being furniture and lighting design.

Over the years I have created hundreds of paintings and designed many products, such as, dog toys and clothes, furniture and a skin care/cosmetic line.

"I believe art transforms our emotions and opens our visual awareness".

Bereniche Aguiar

Art and Shop Website: www.berenicheaguiar.com

Recommendations

I recommend only using colored pencils to prevent any color bleed through on the pages. I also suggest putting a piece of cardboard underneath the page being colored, for more support, if it is desired to press hard with the colored pencils.

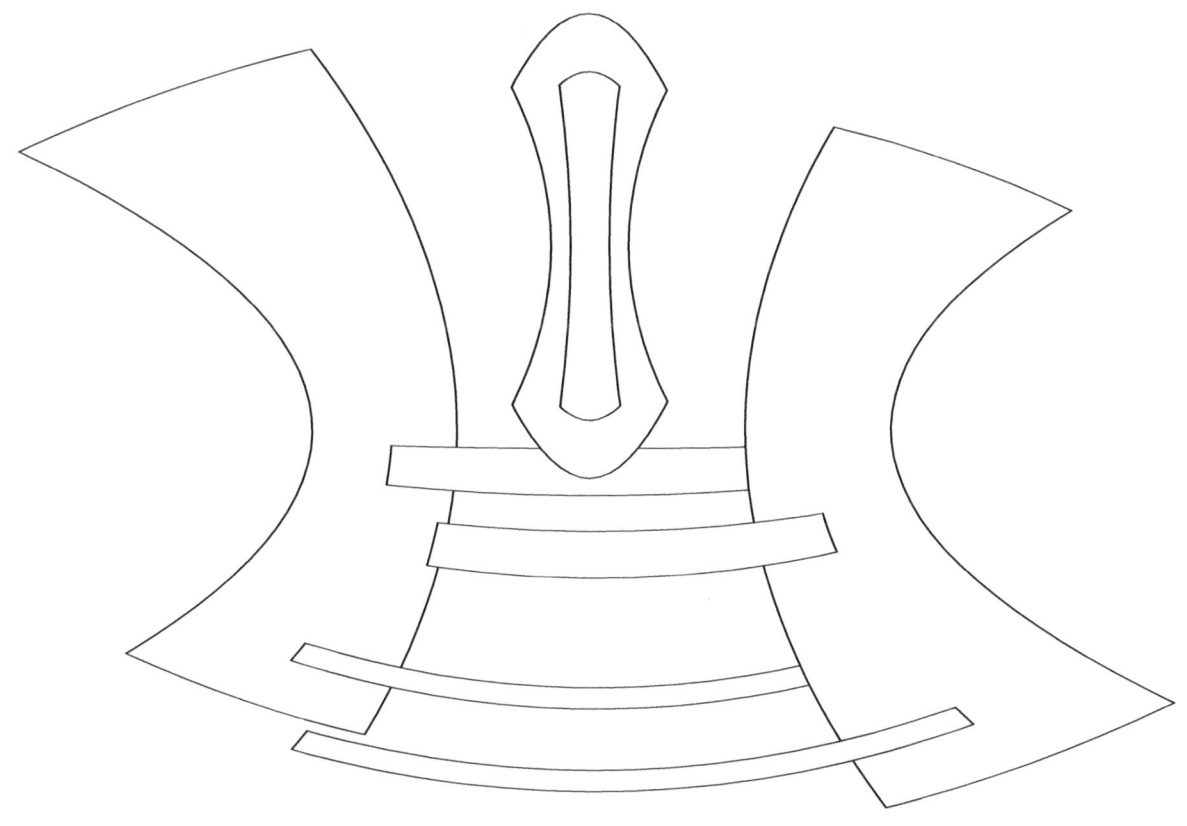

The full size drawing is on page 33

D#   9

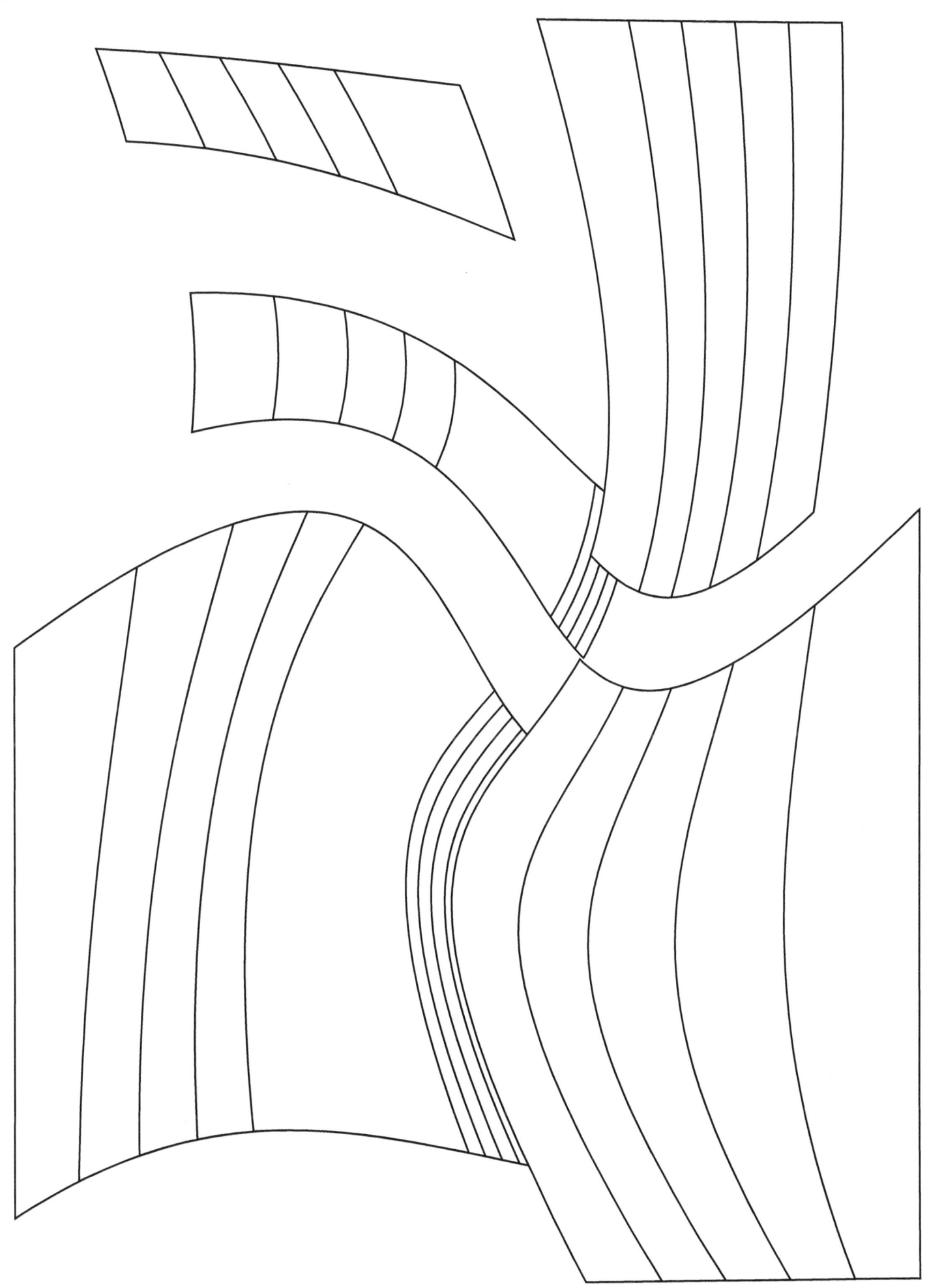

D# 78

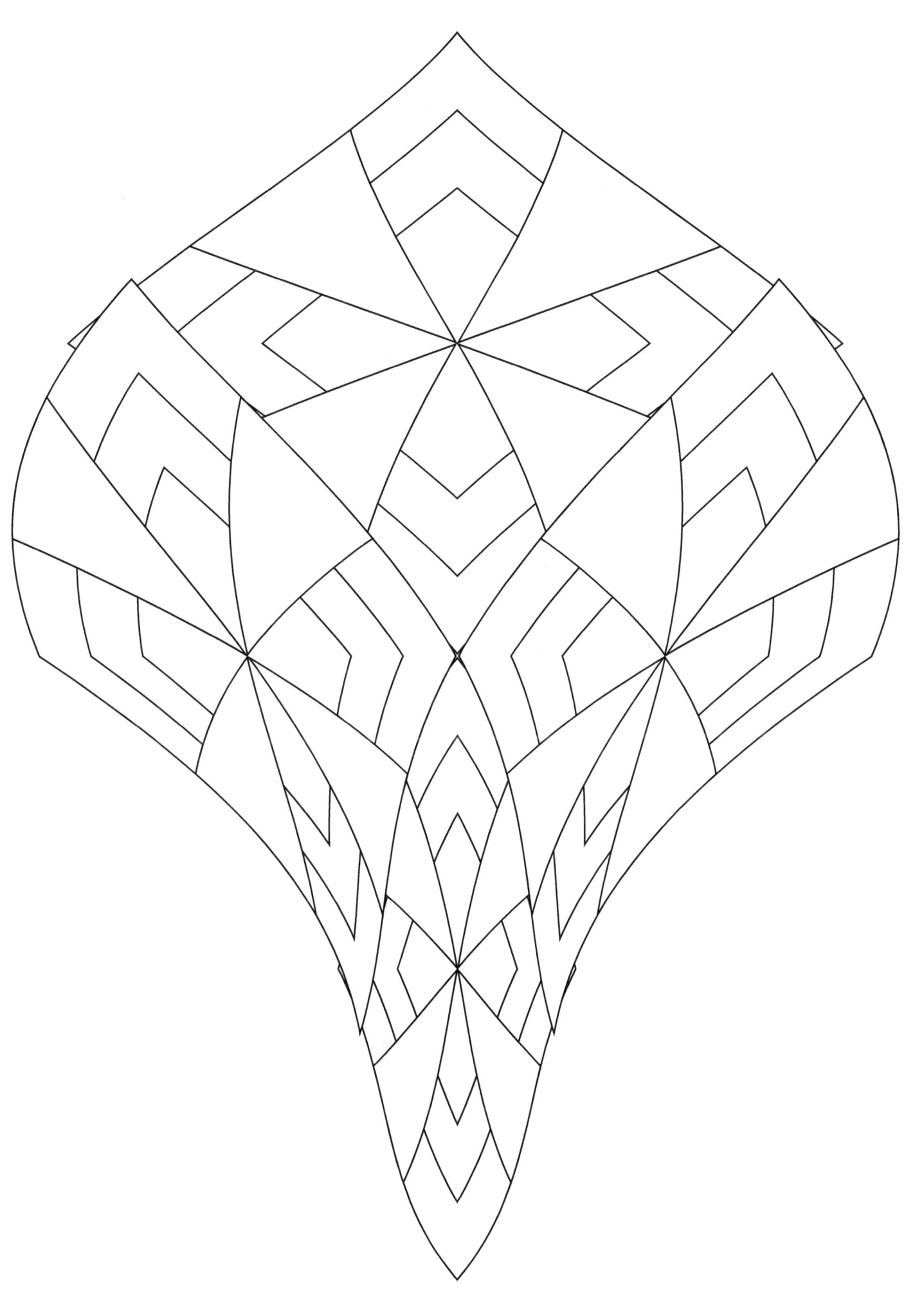

D#   7

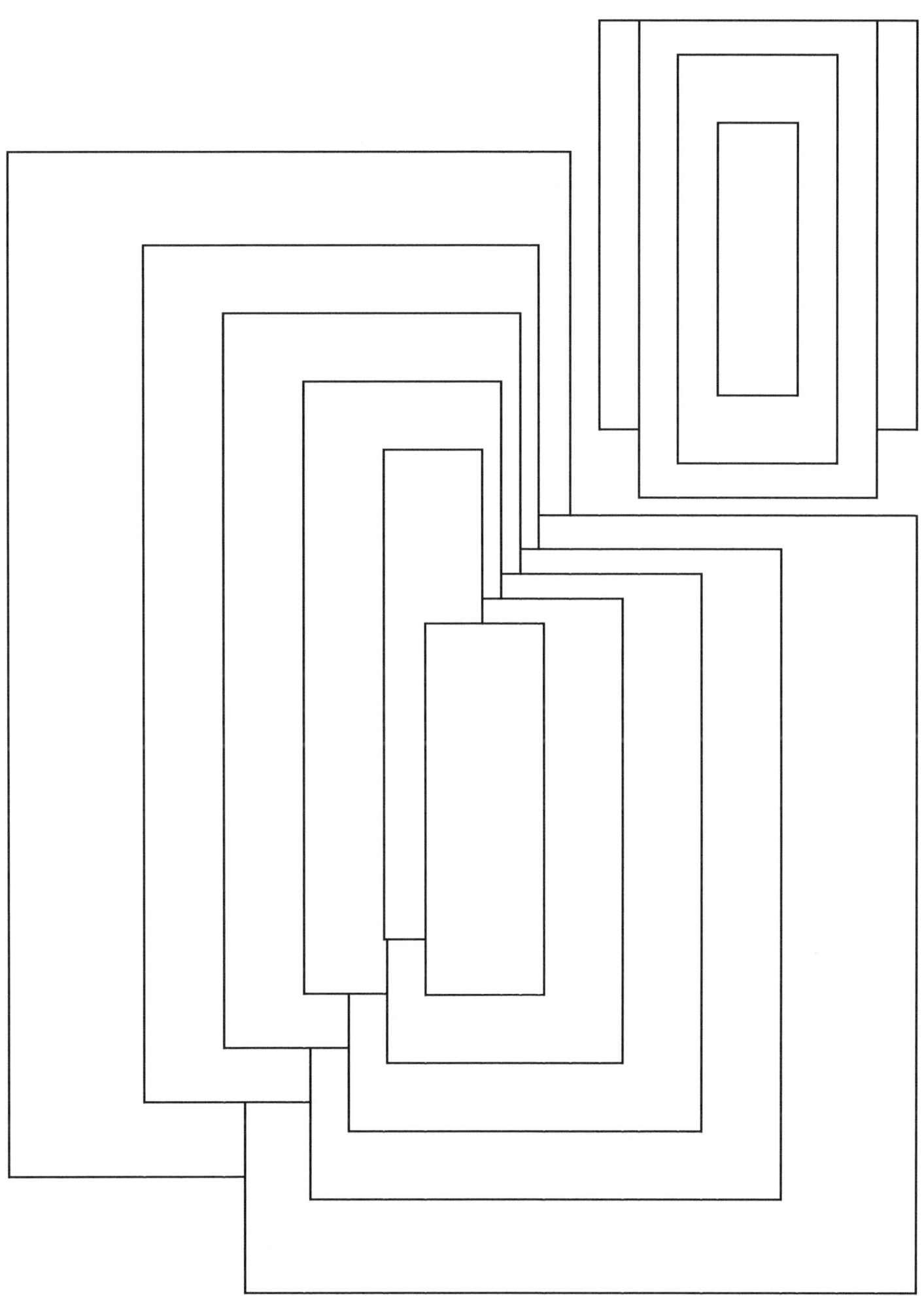

D#   8

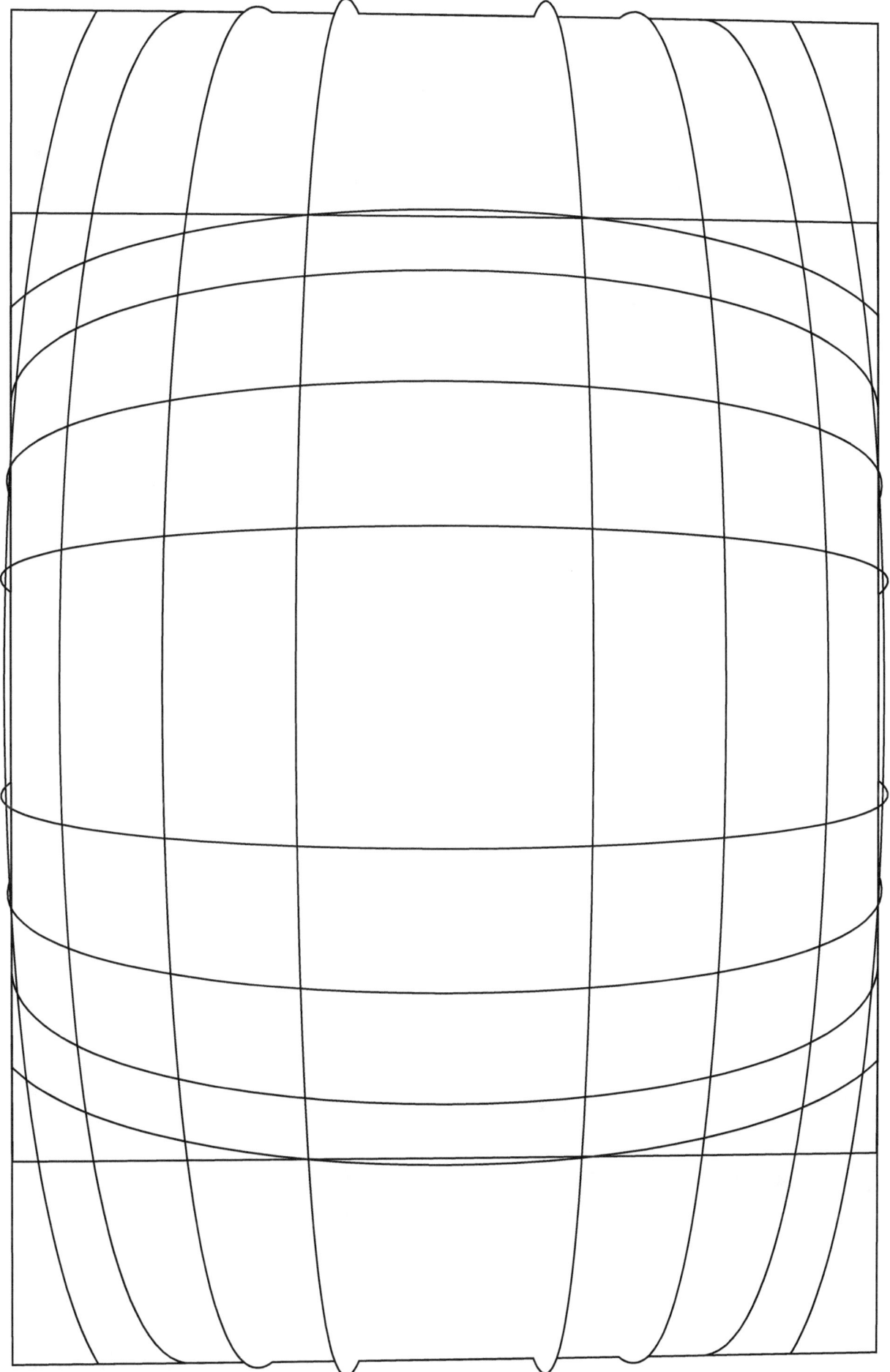

D#   71

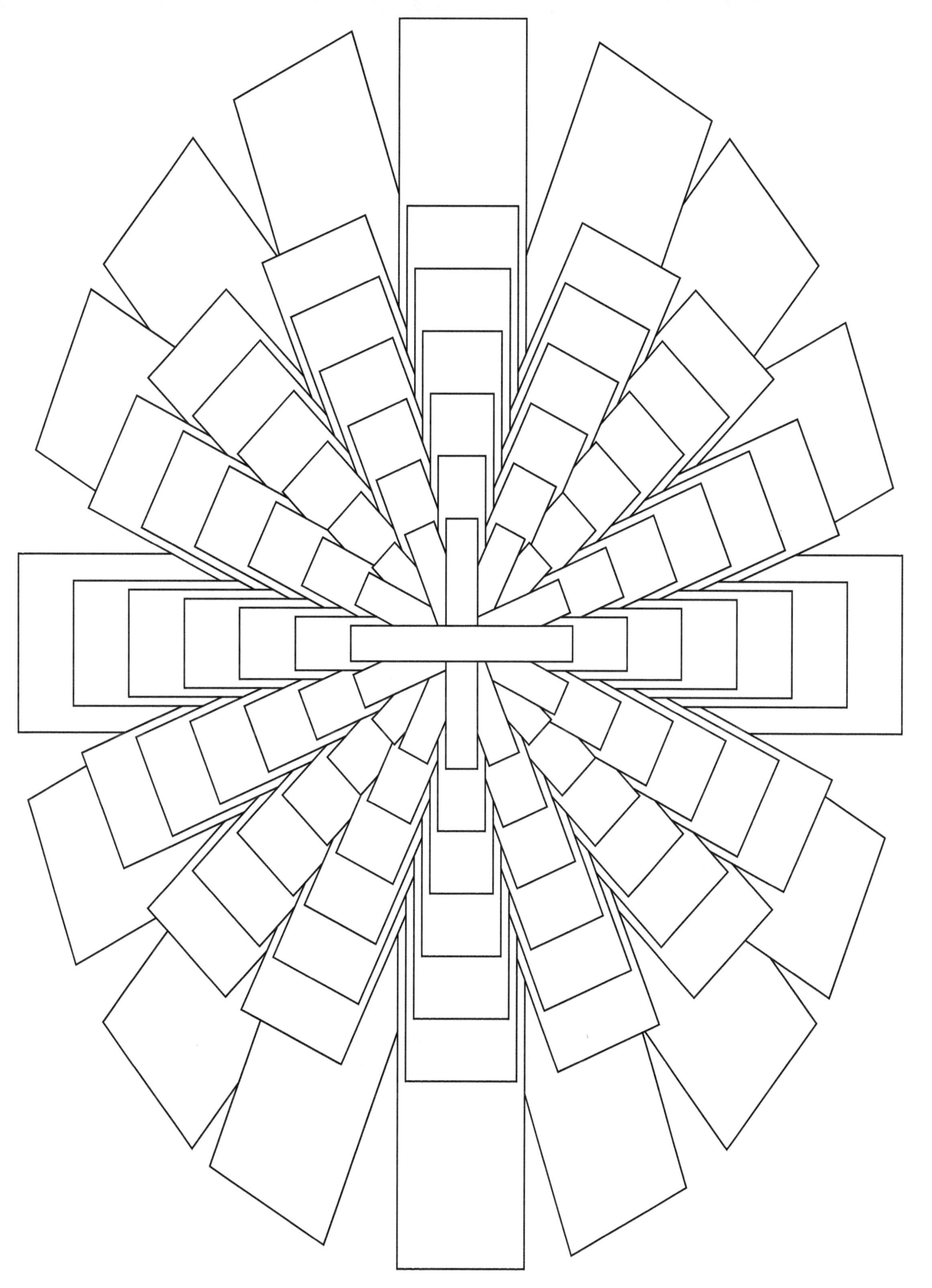

D#   10

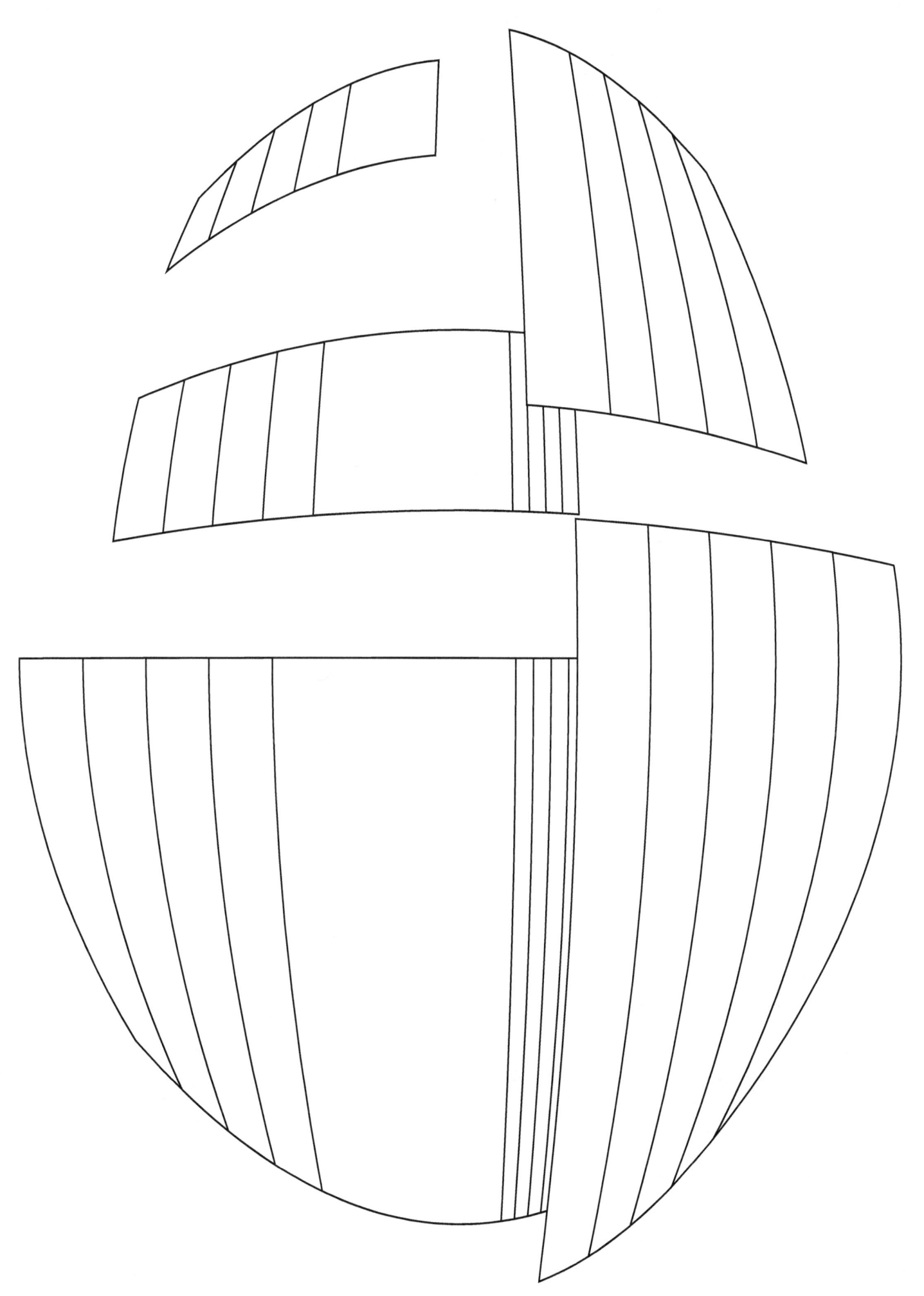

D# 11

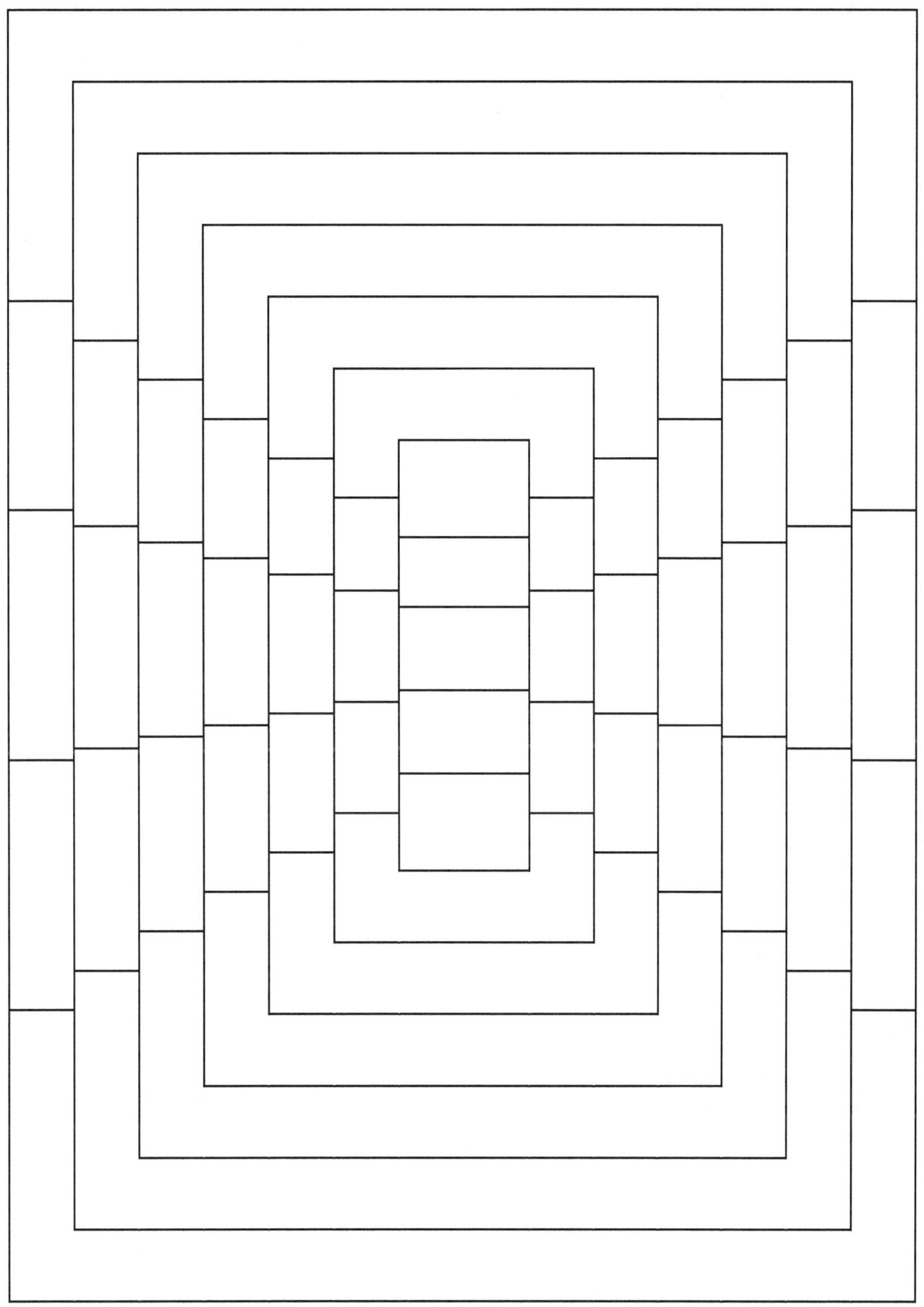

D#   12

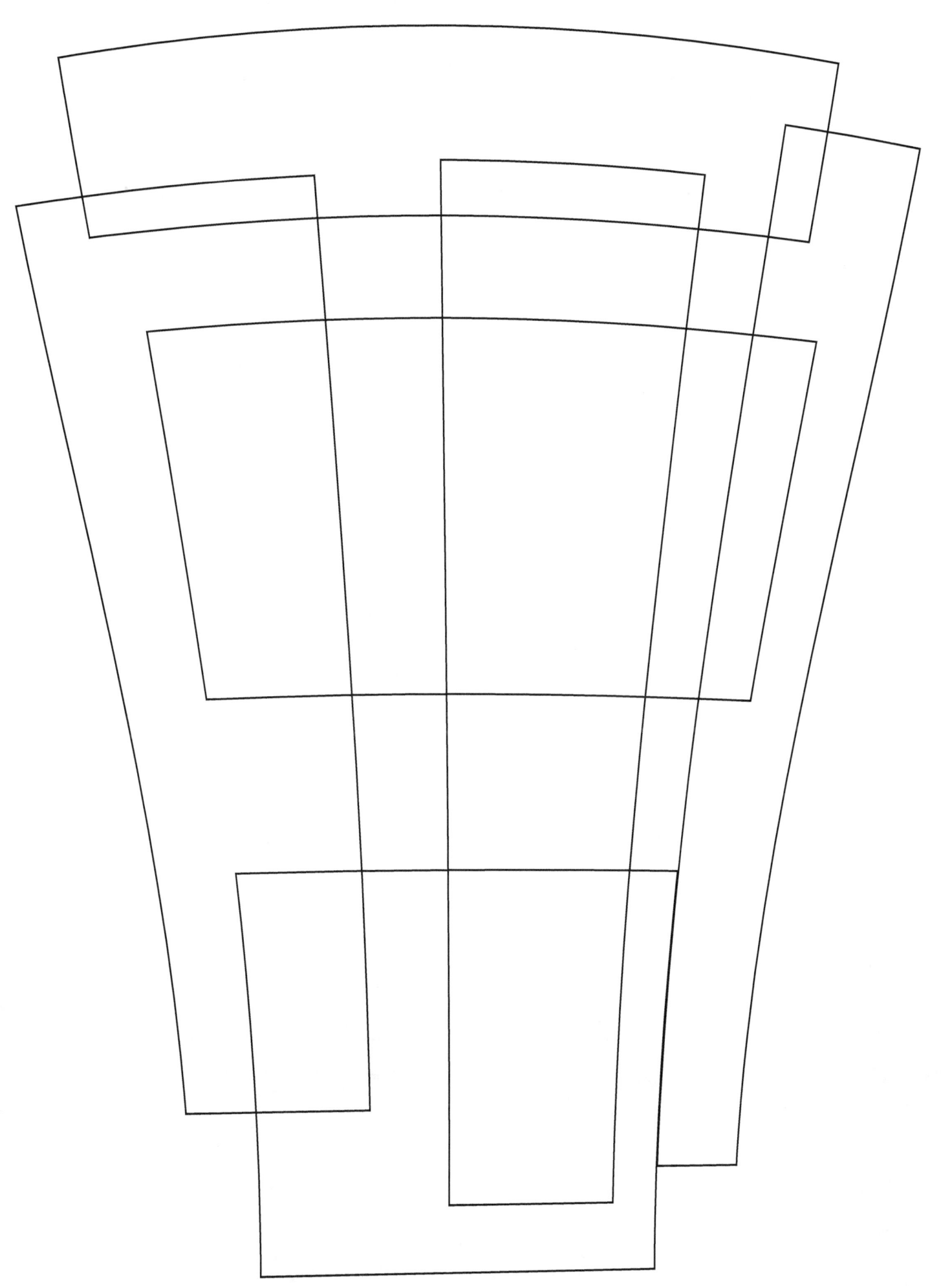

D#   14

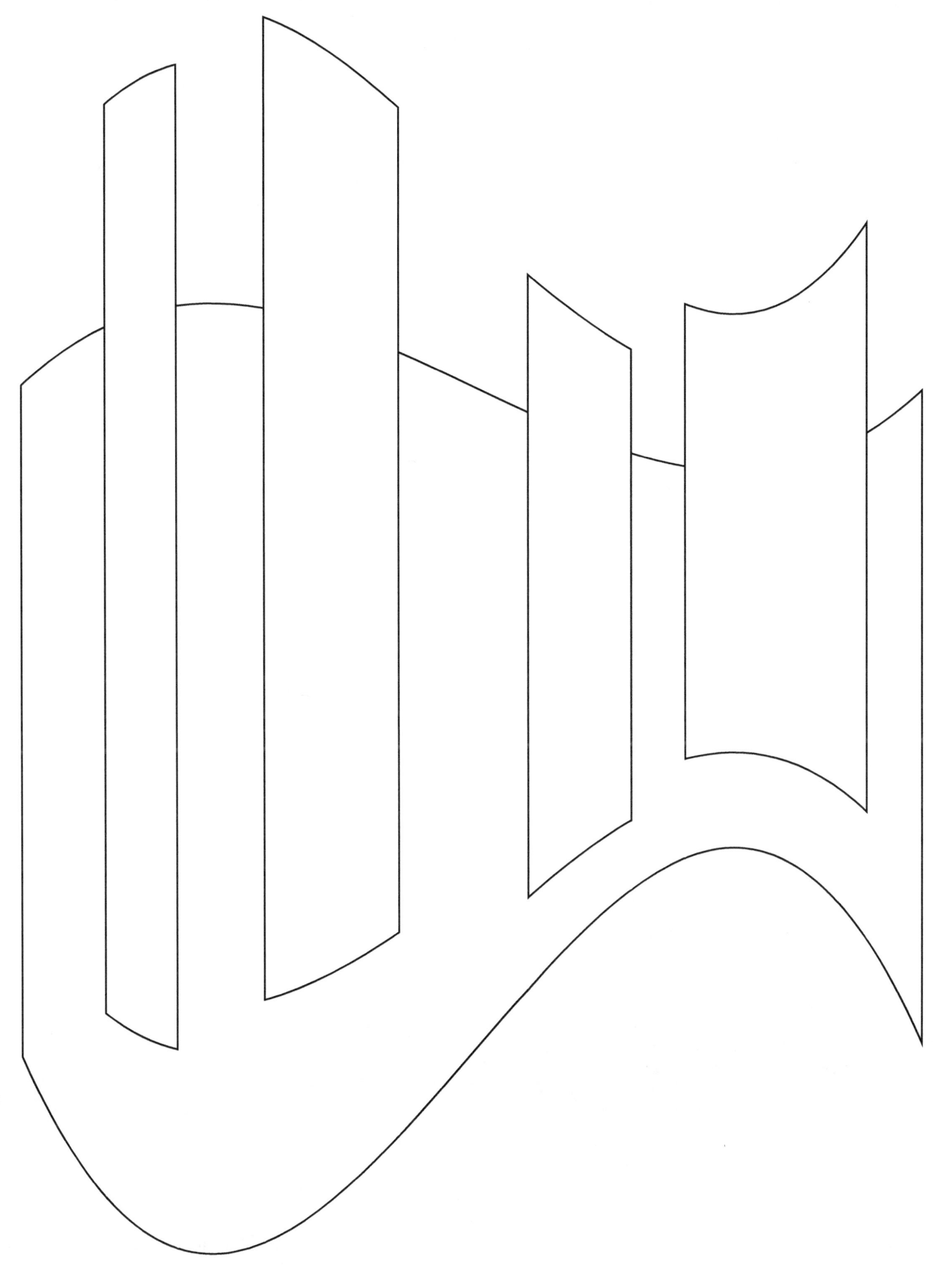

D#   15

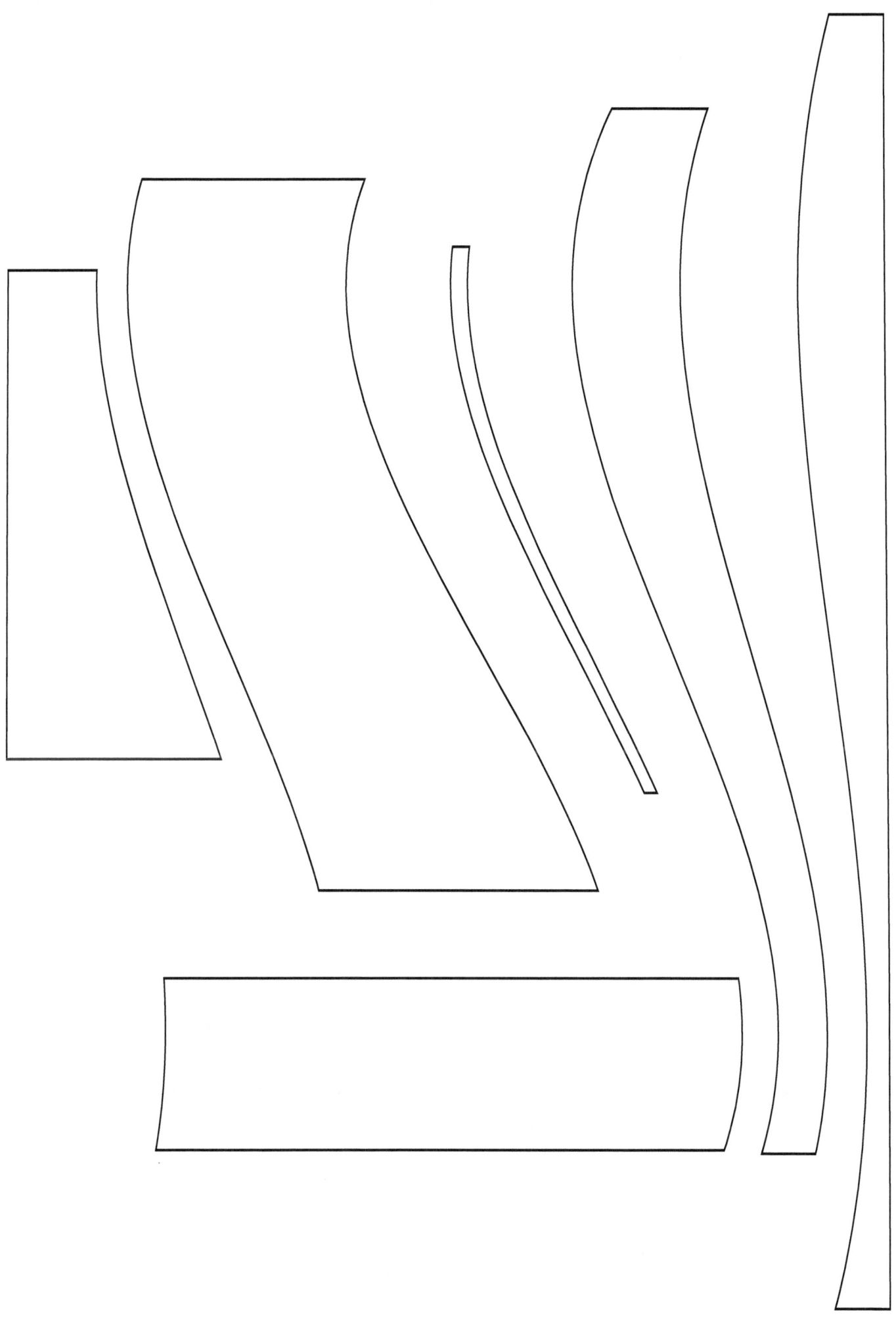

D# 16

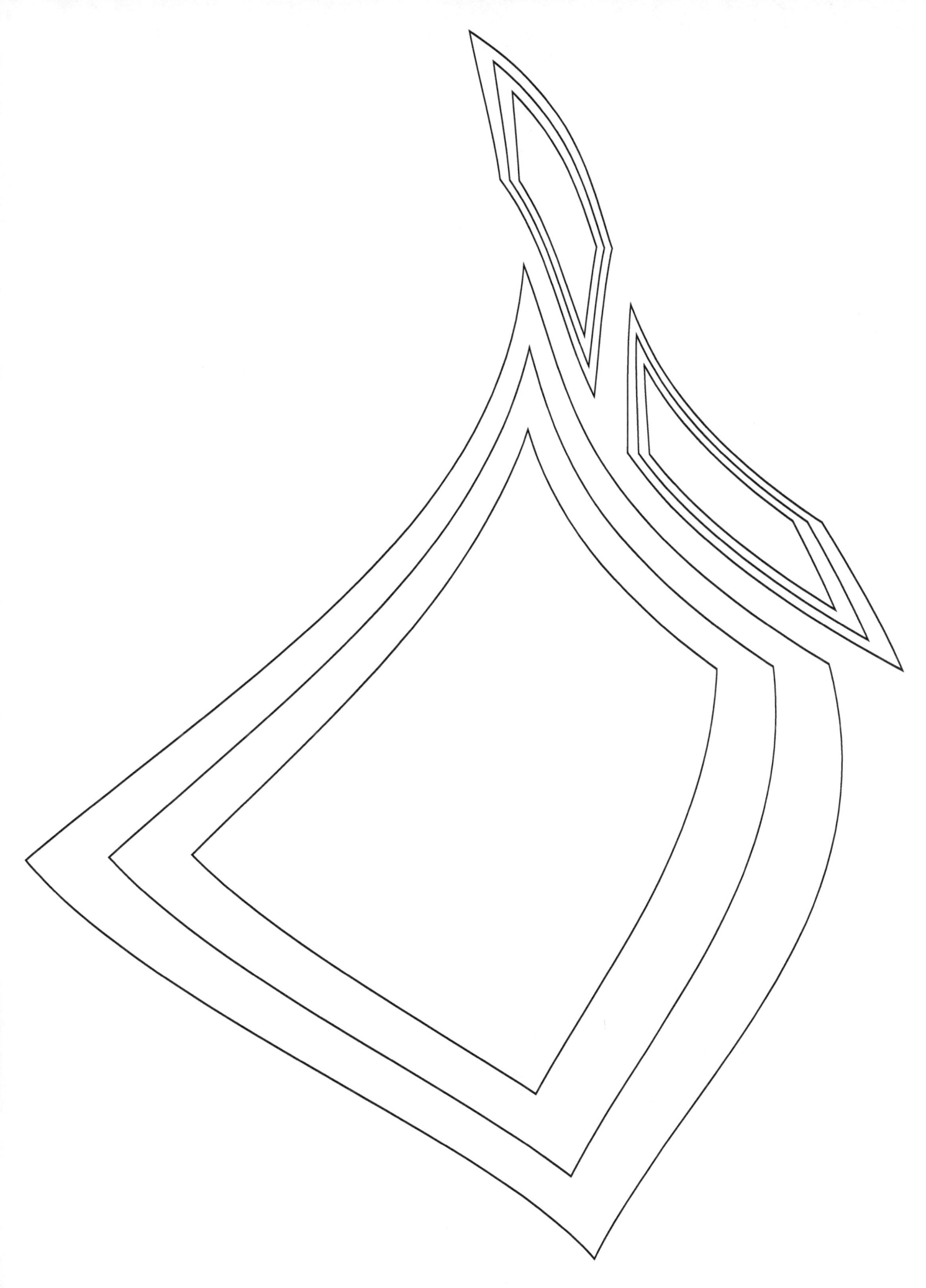

D# 109

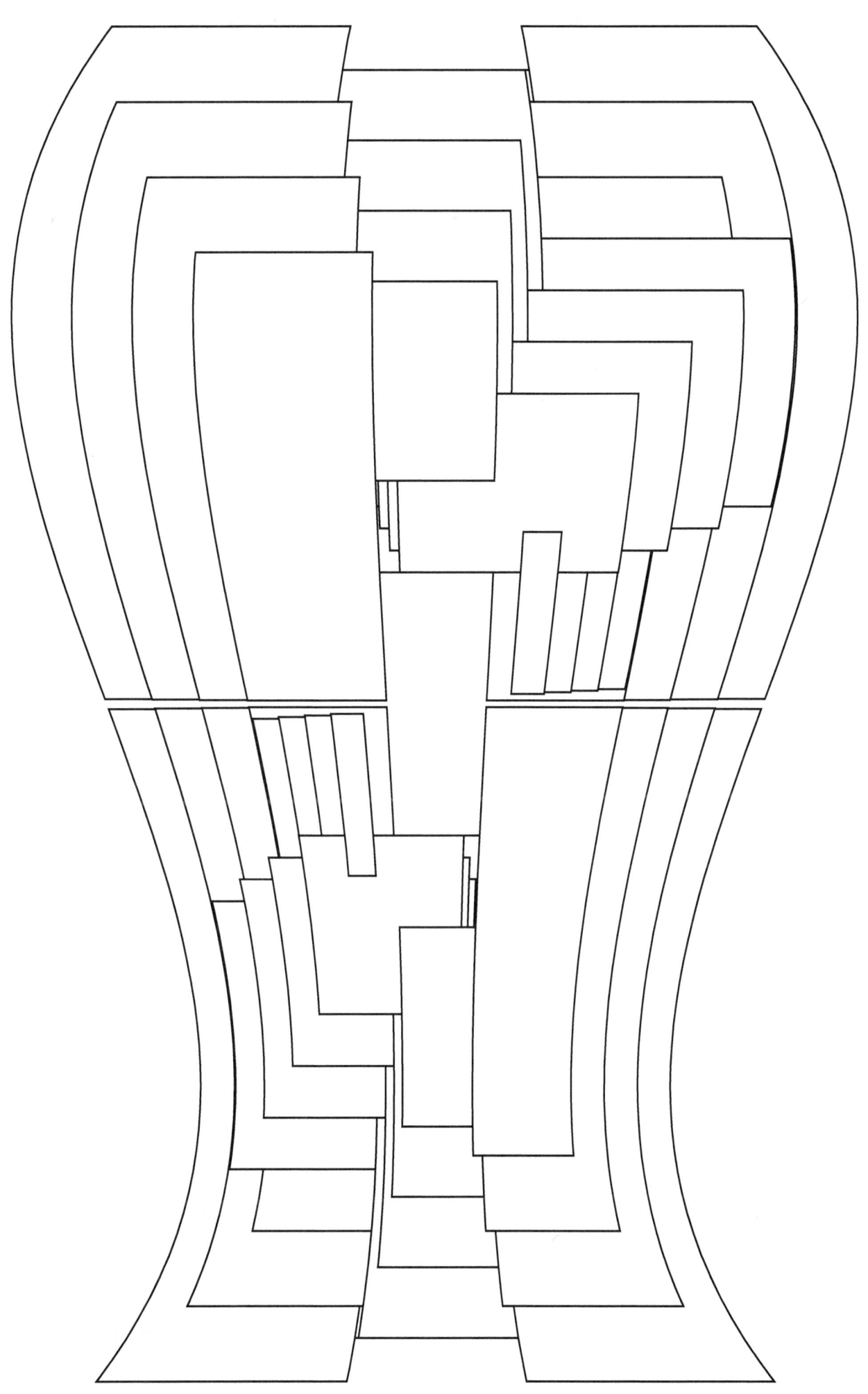

D# 19

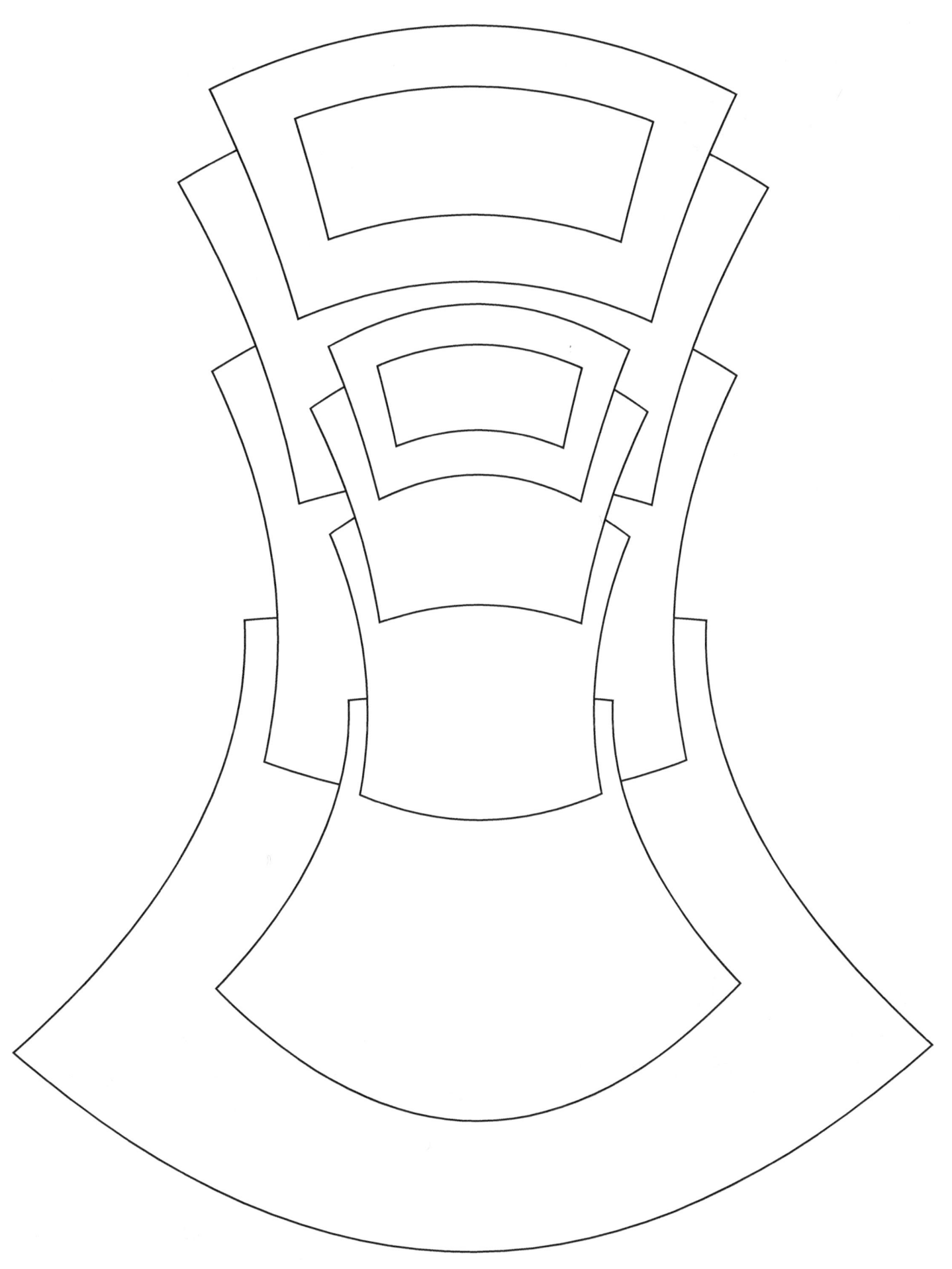

D# 20

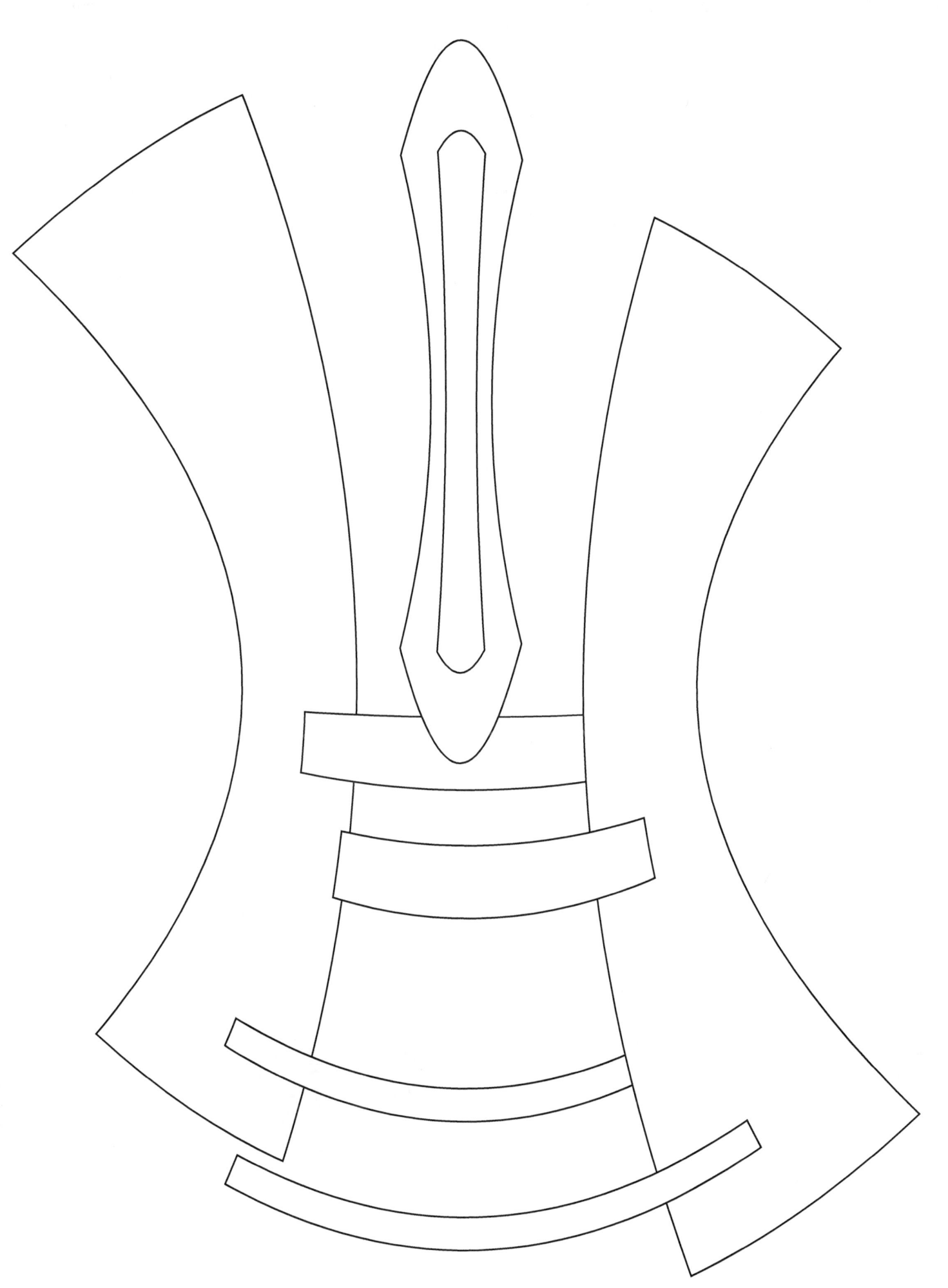

D#   21

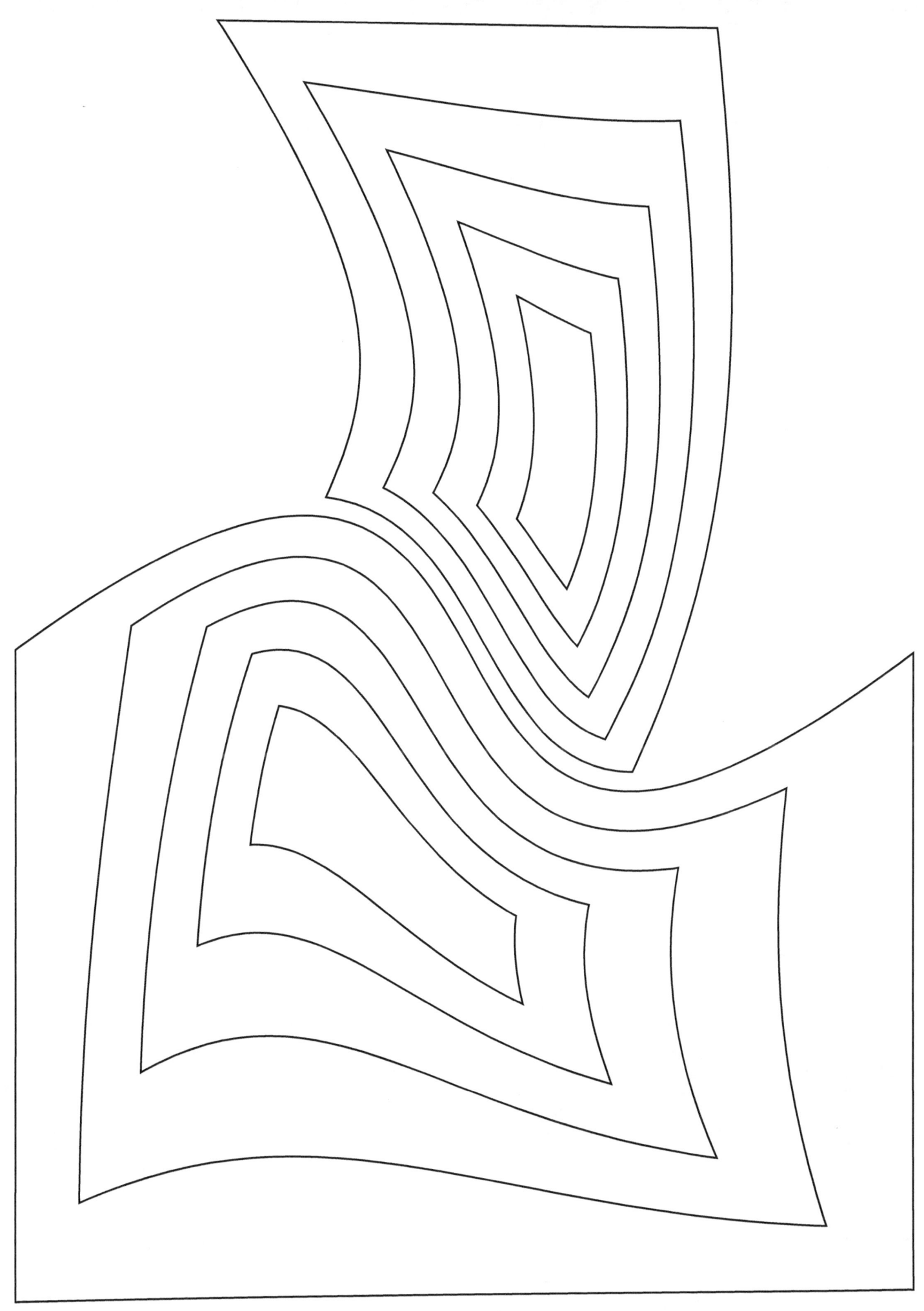

D# 80

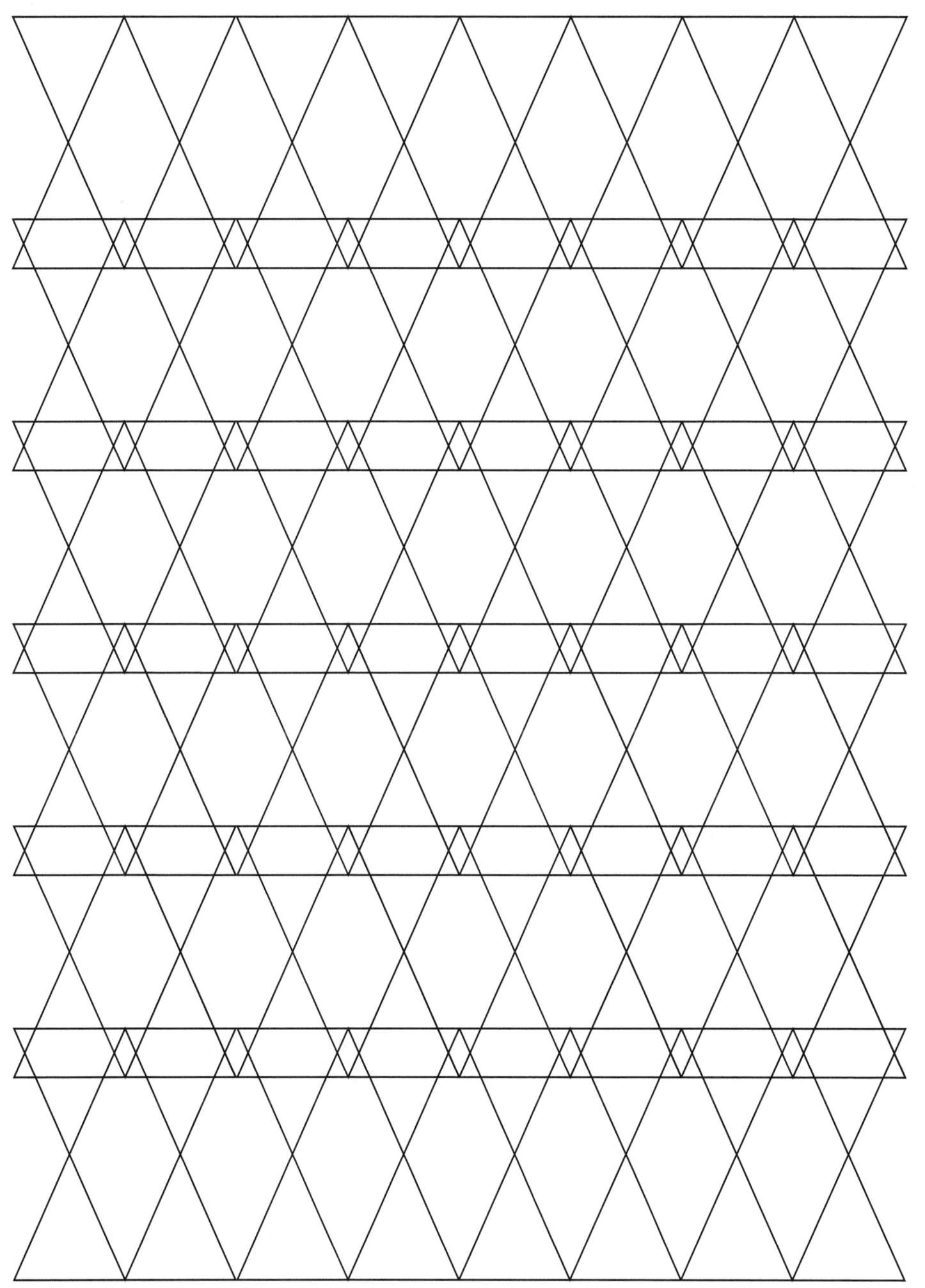

D# 24

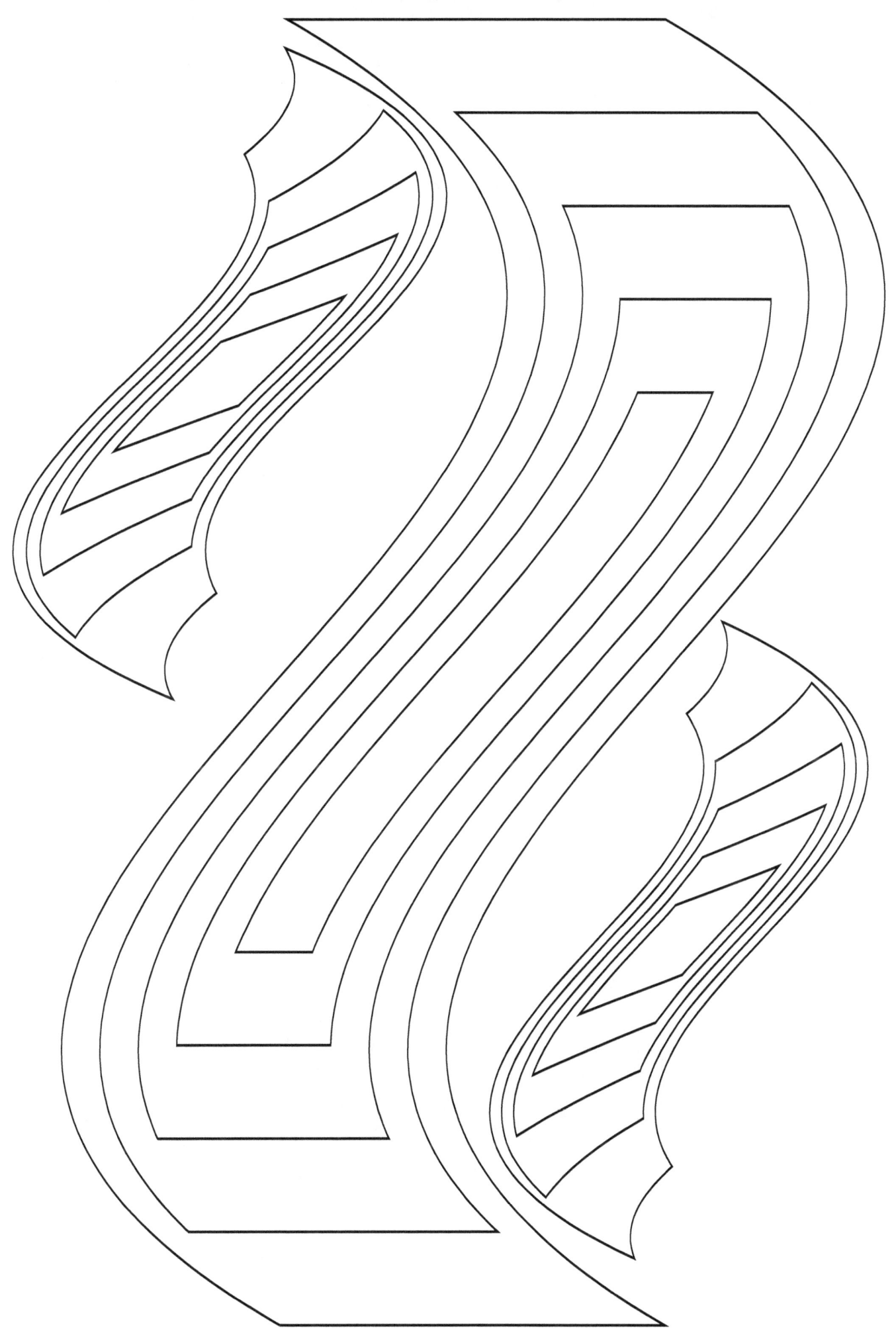

D# 57

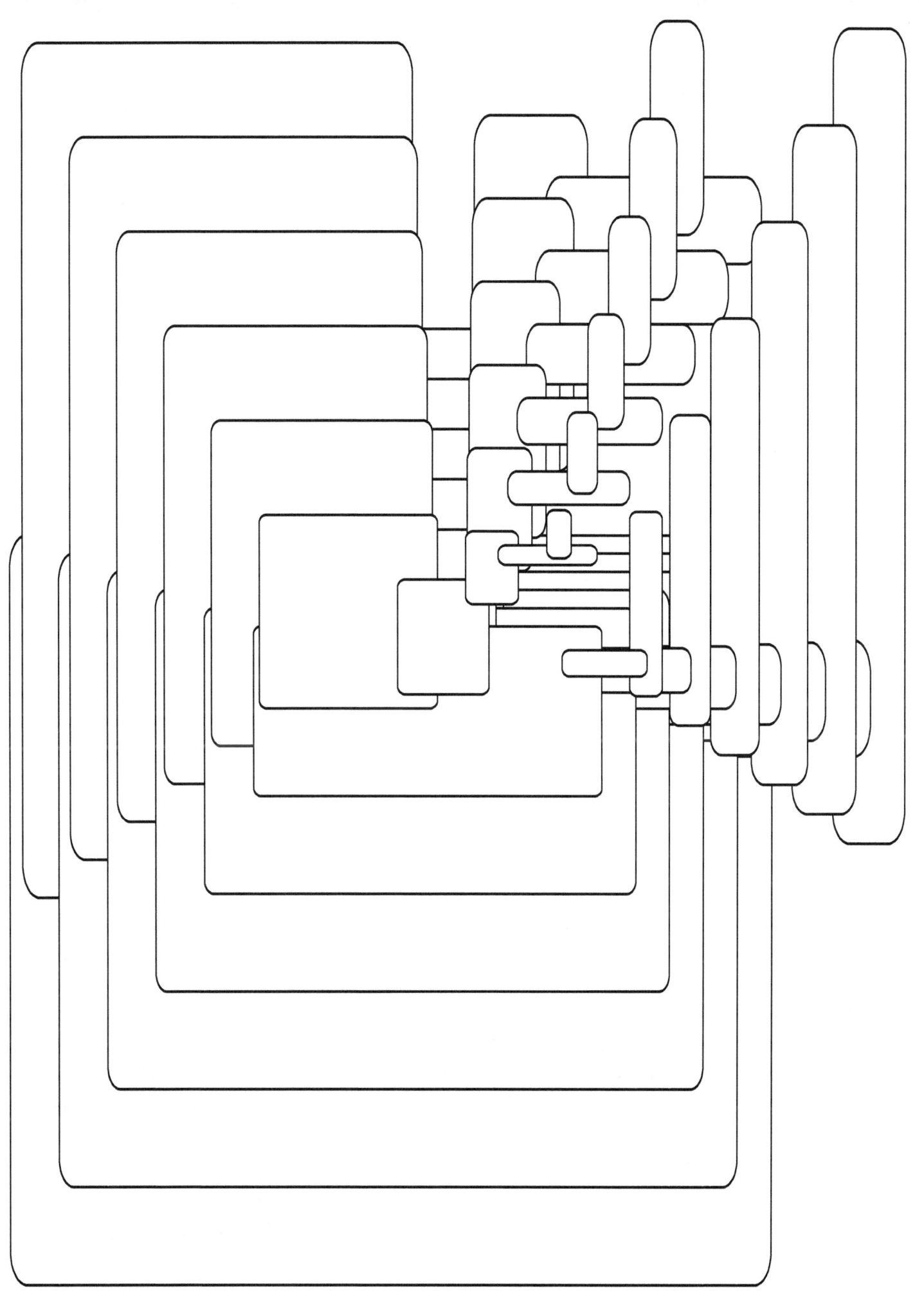

D# 79

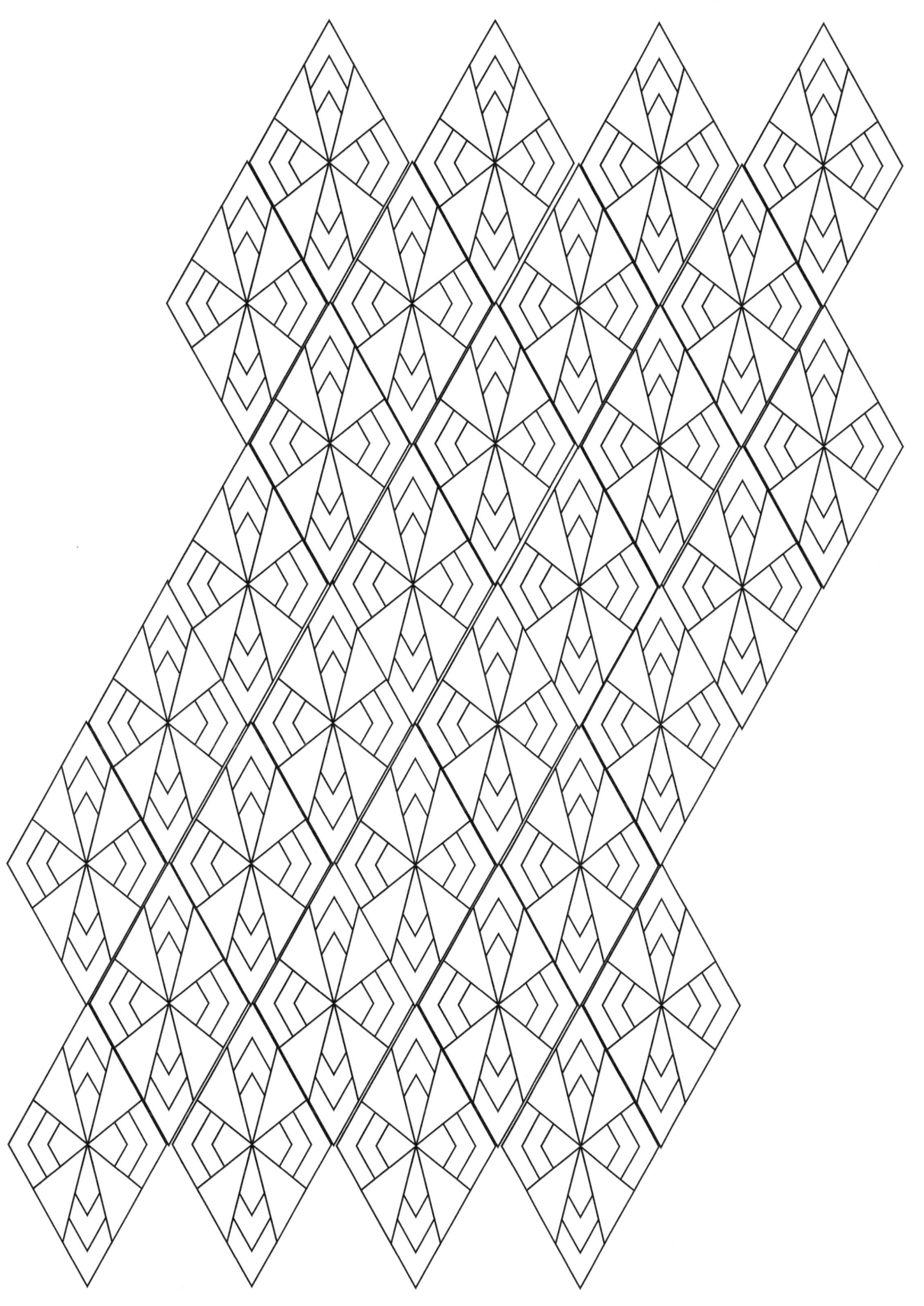

D# 26

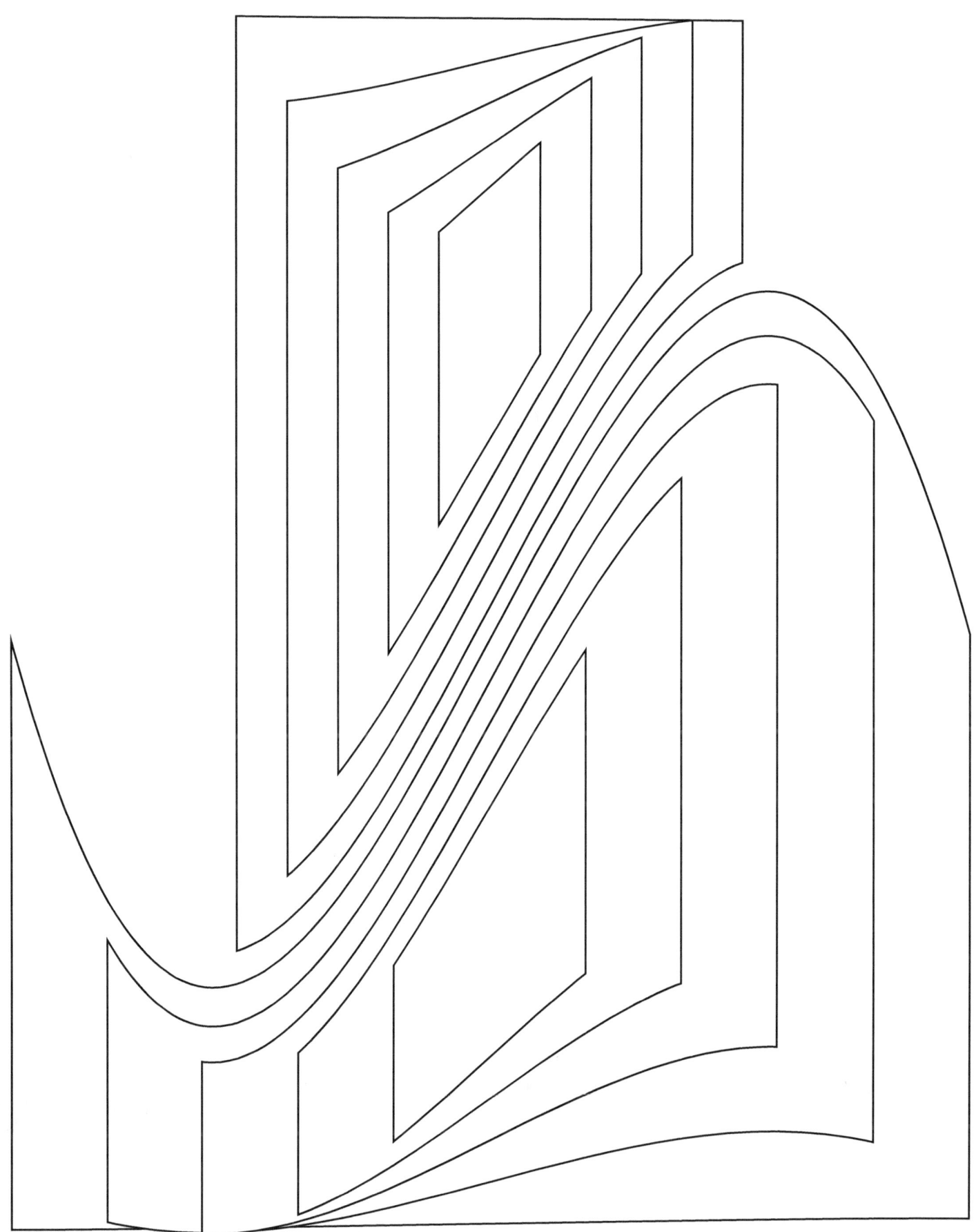

D#   27

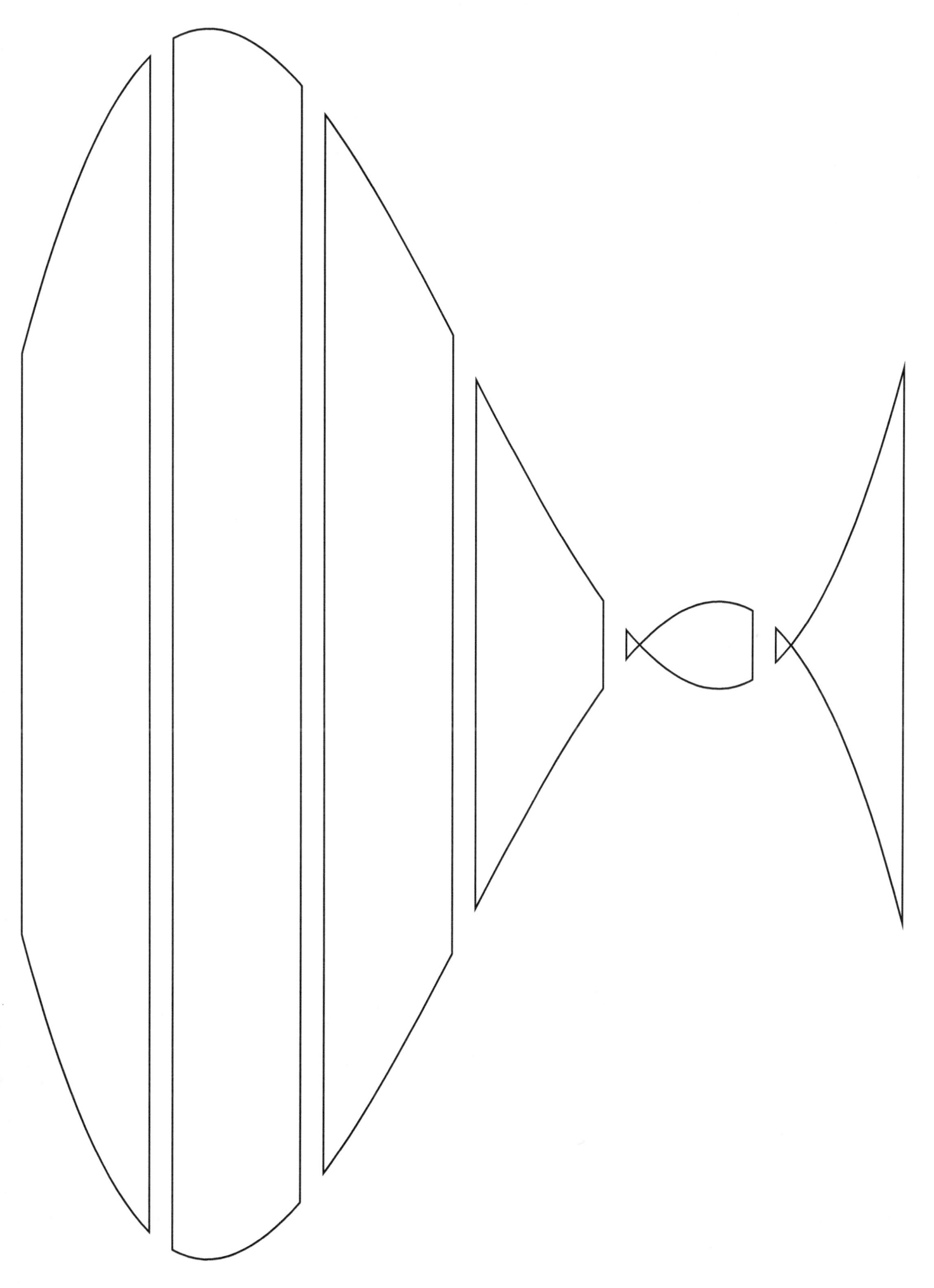

D# 28

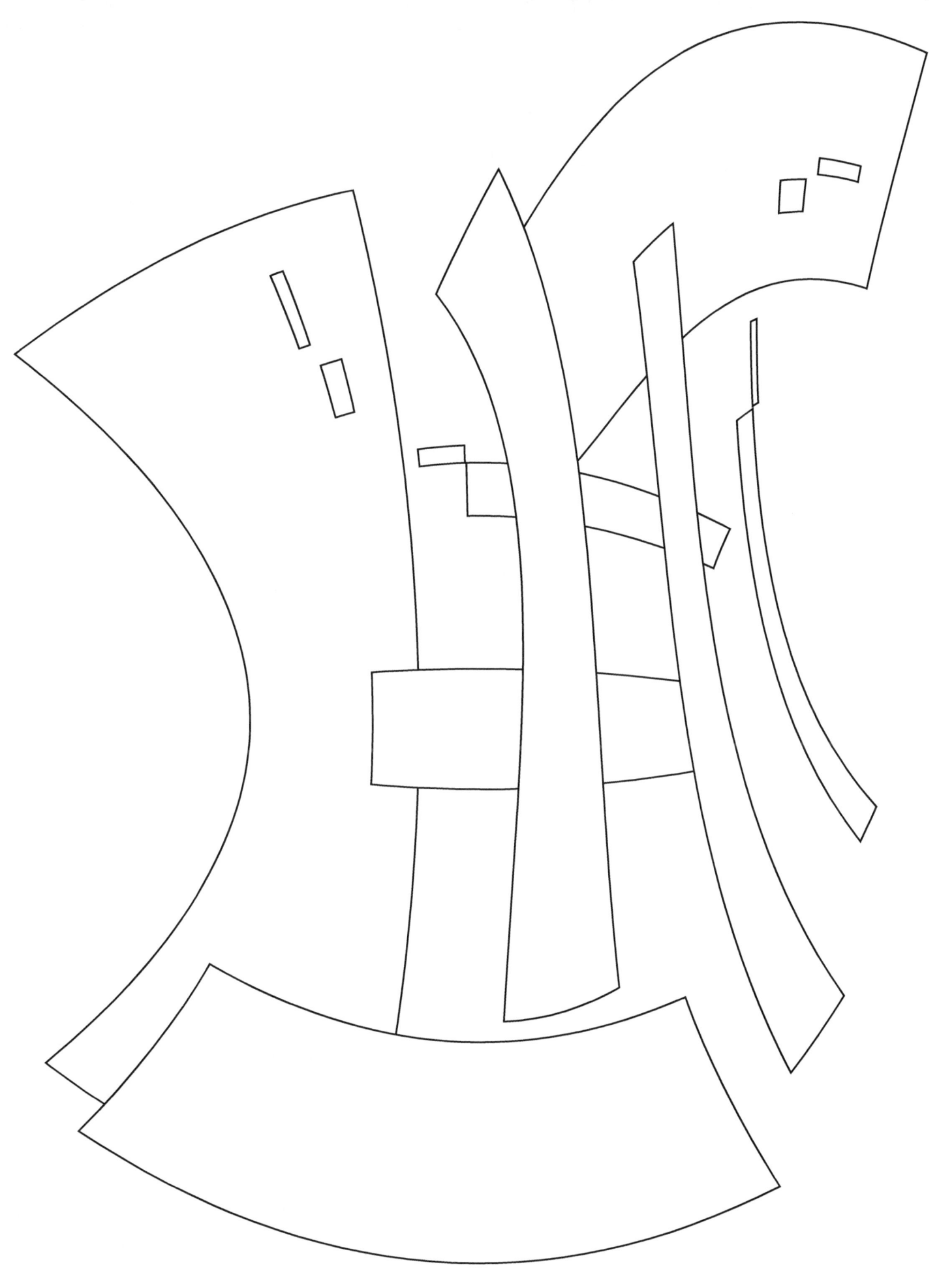

D# 84

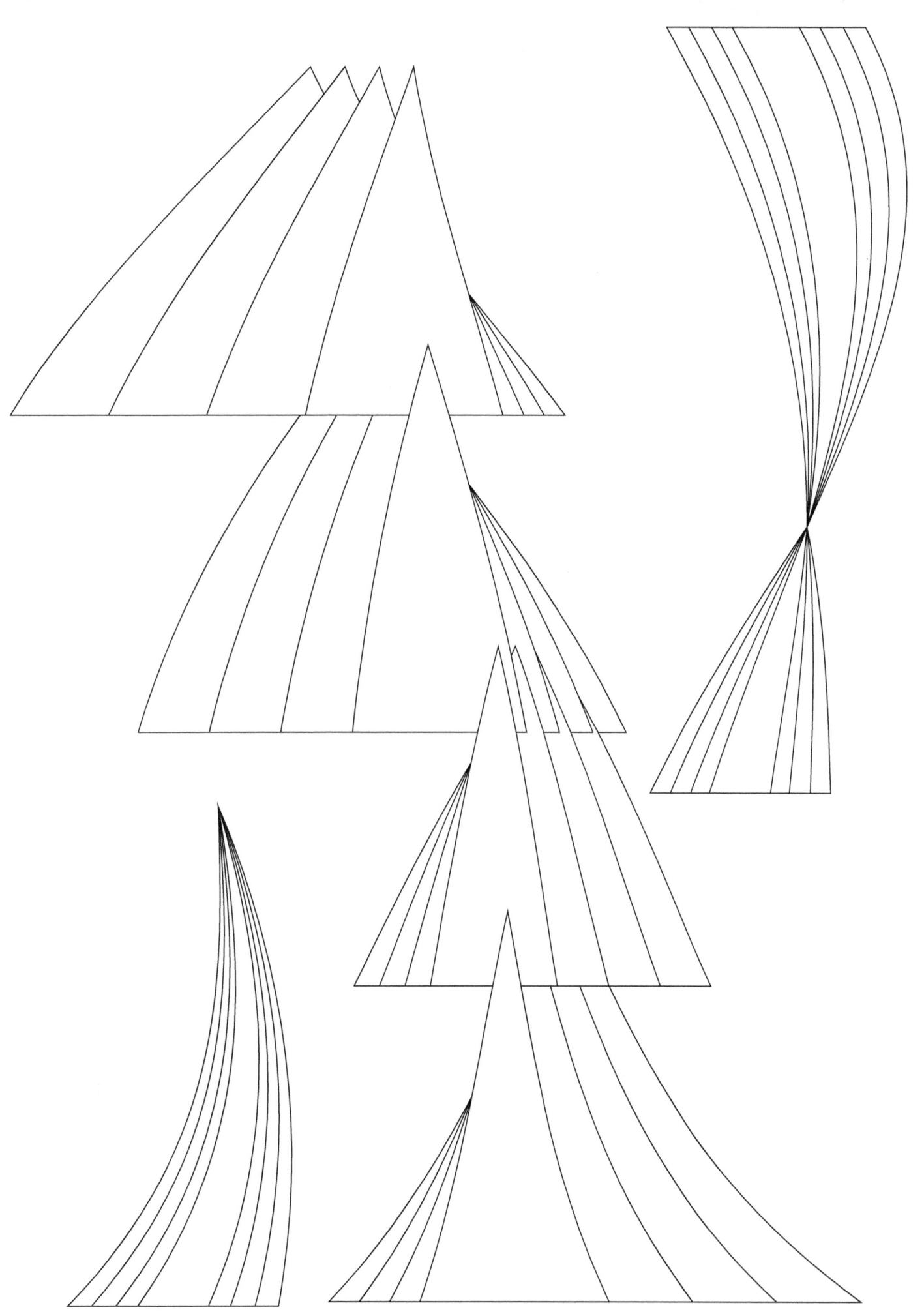

D# 107

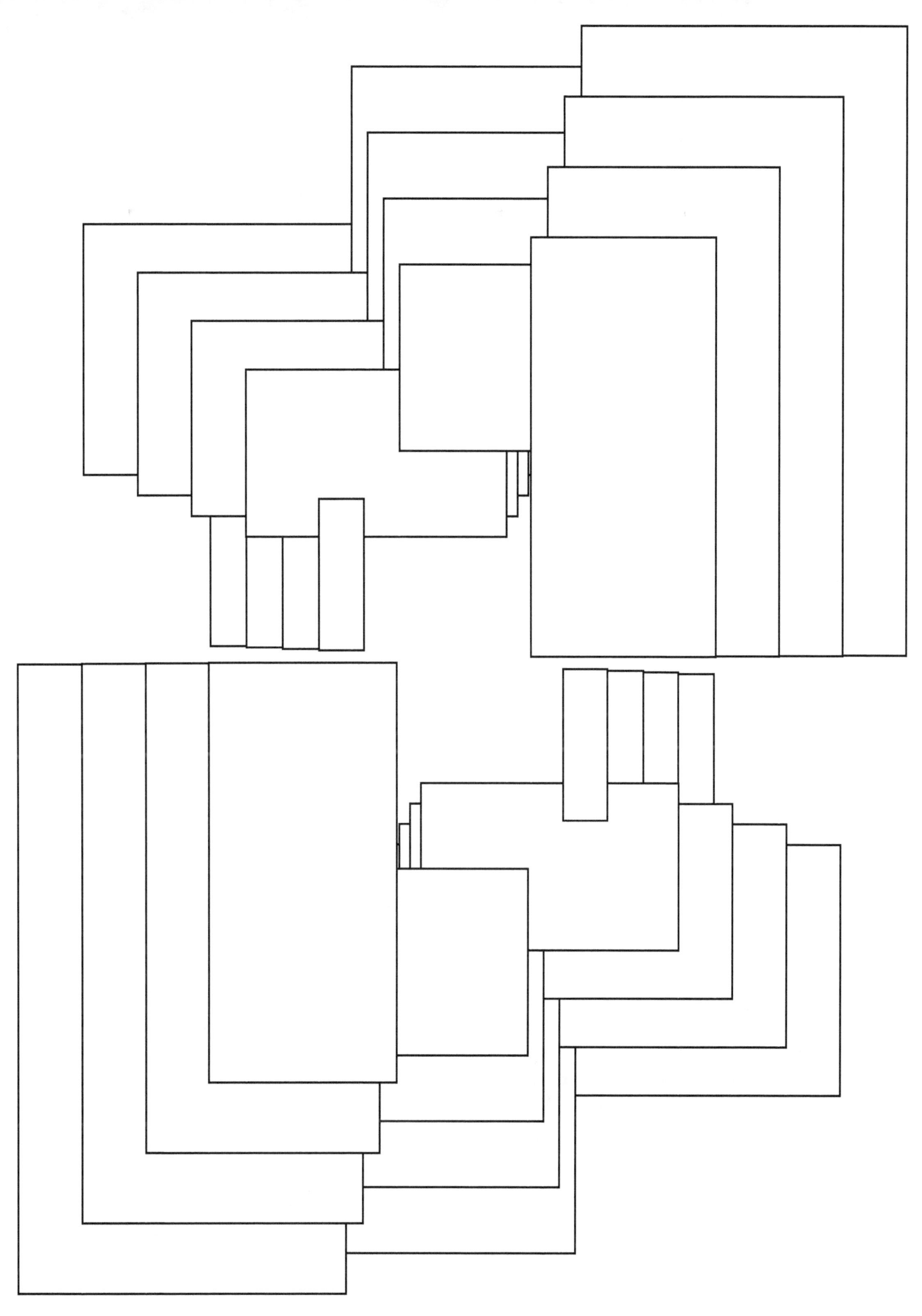

D#   31

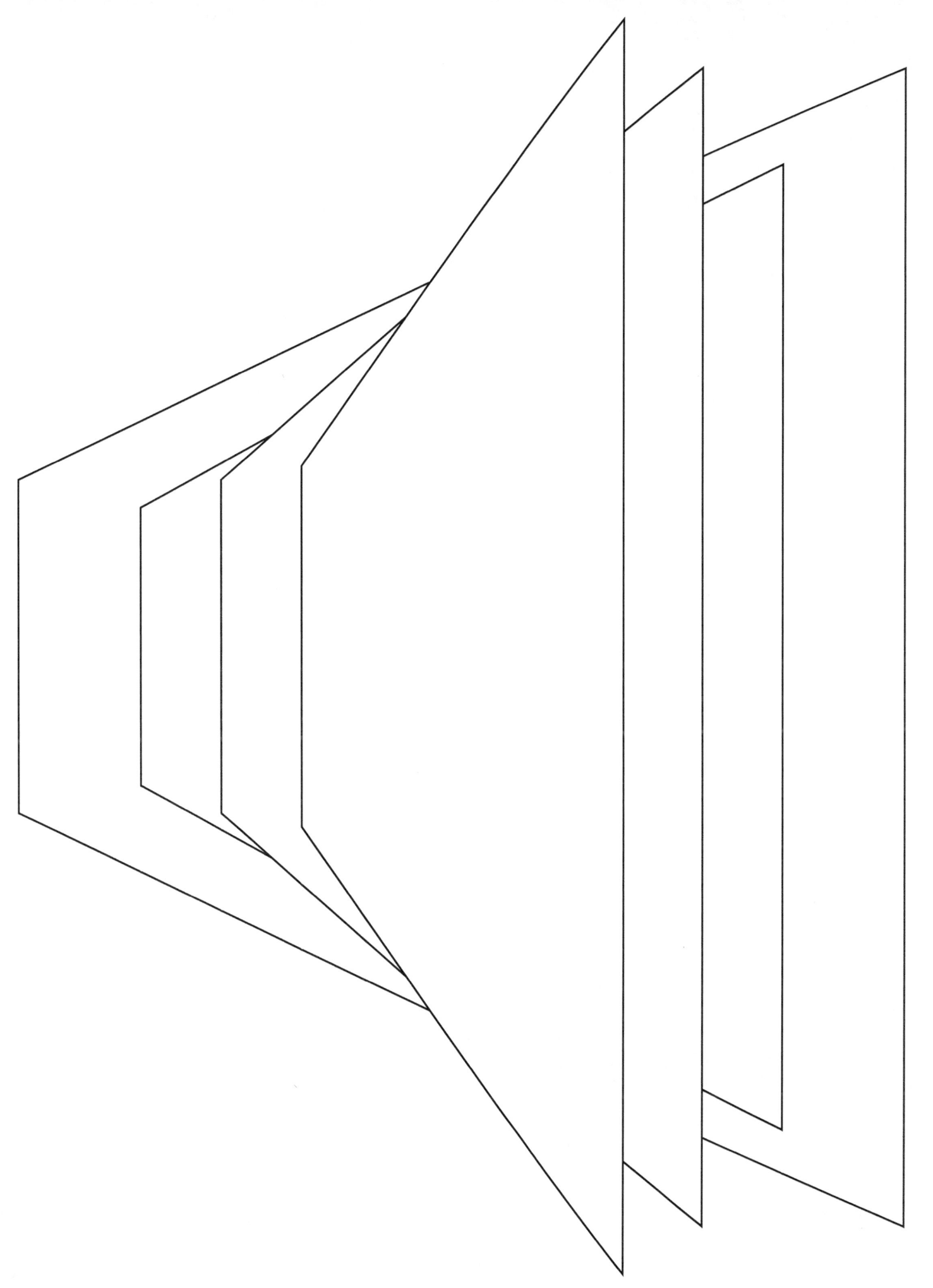

D# 105

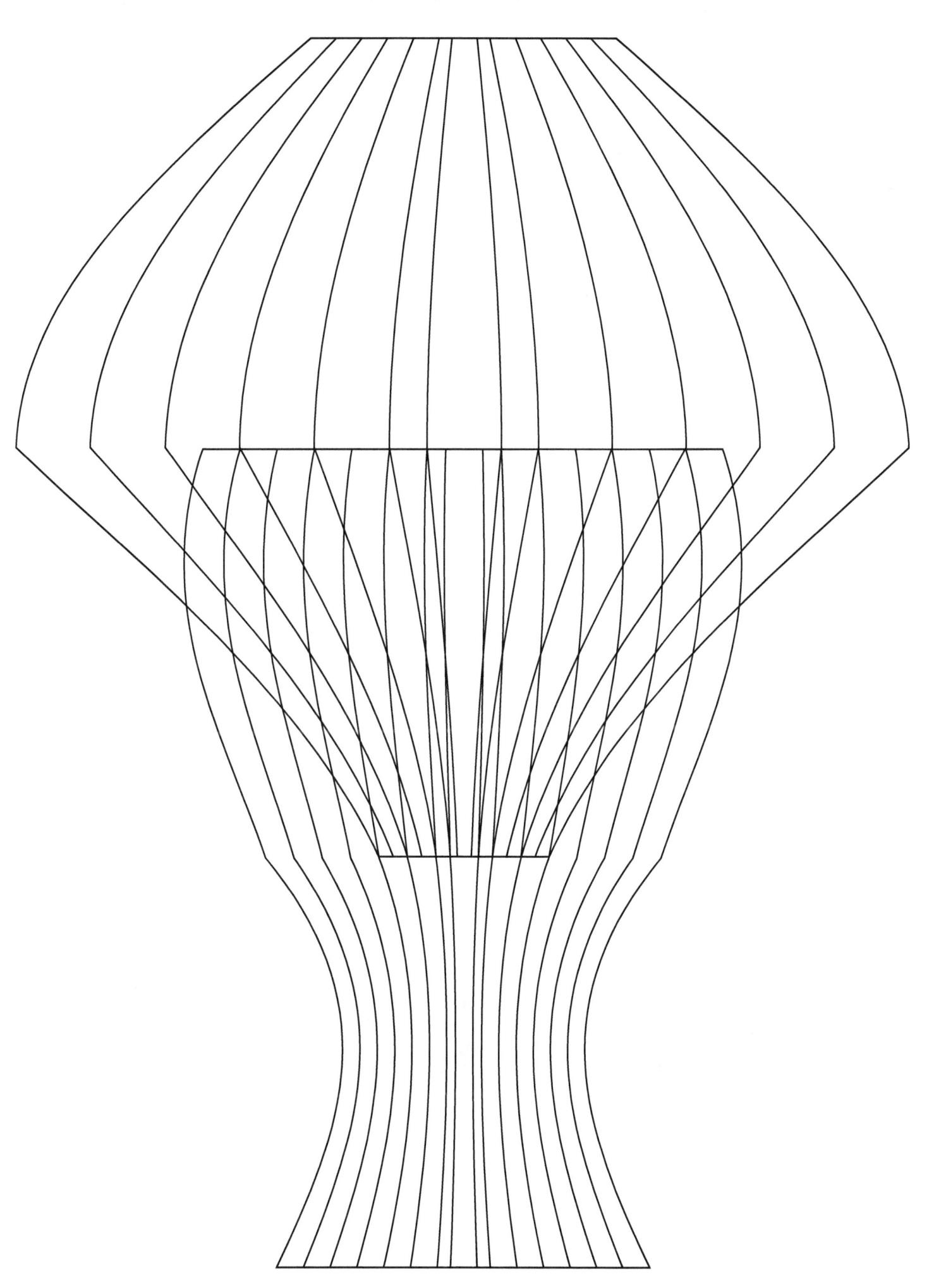

D#   37

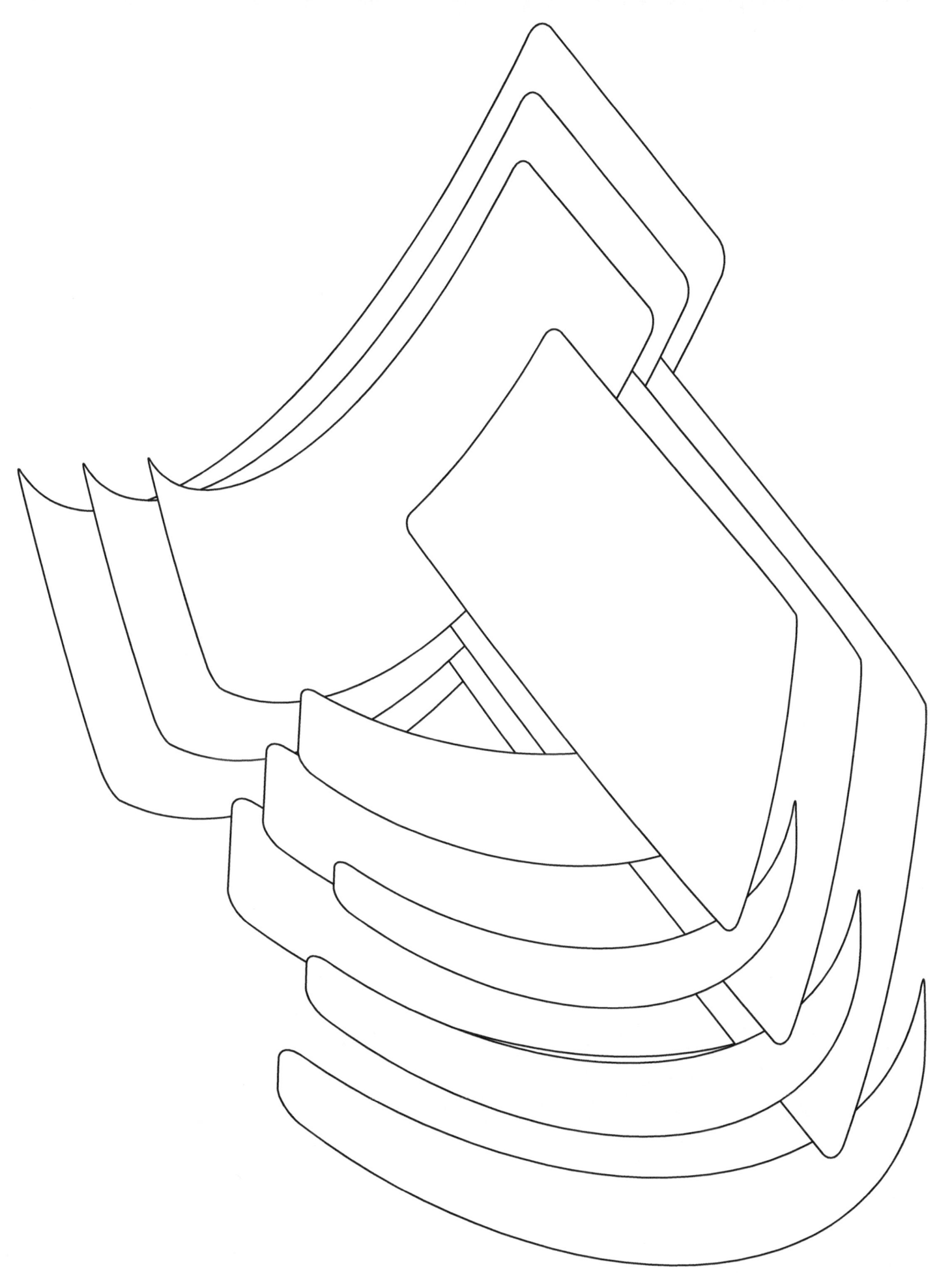

D#   40

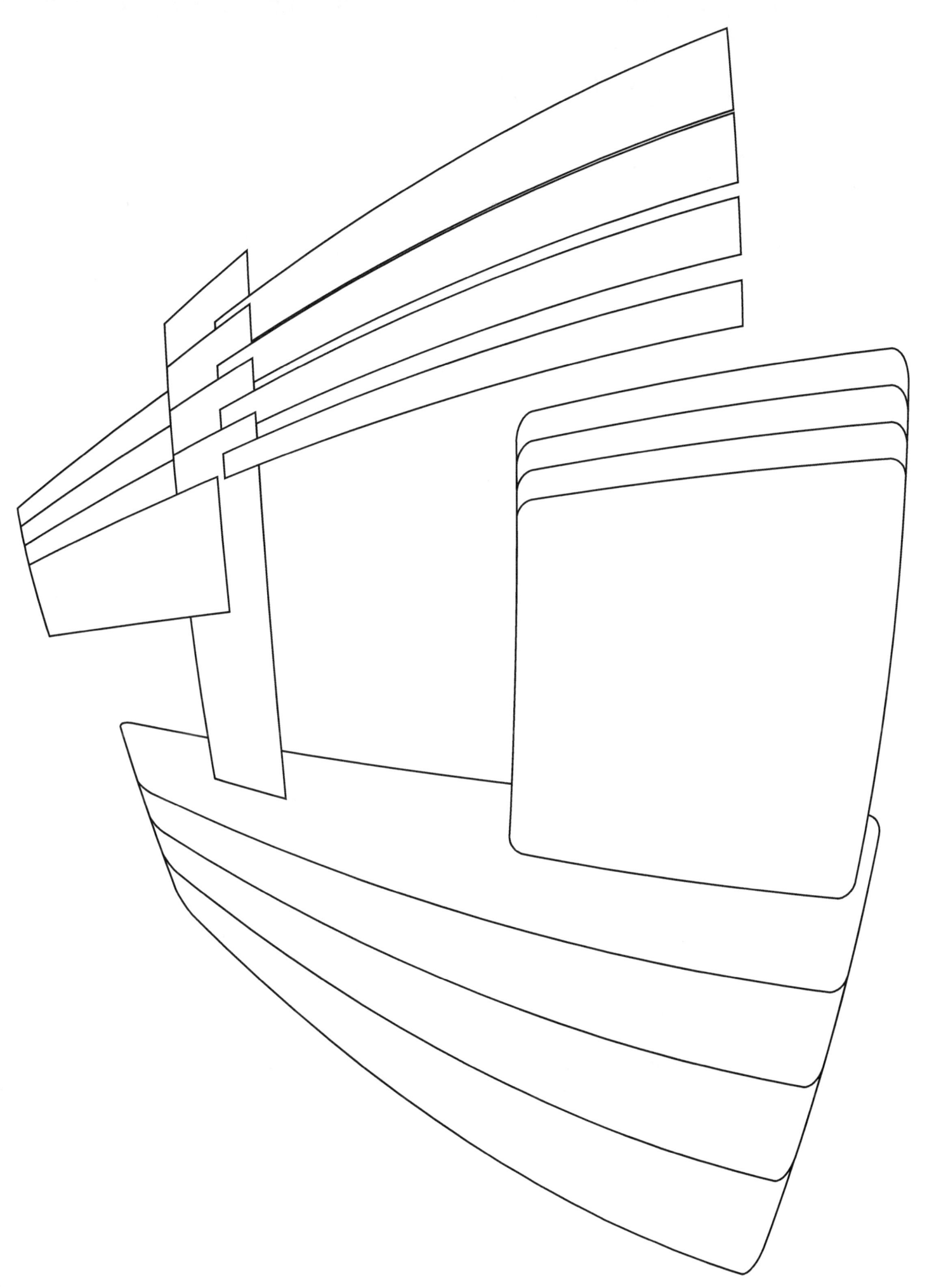

D#   89

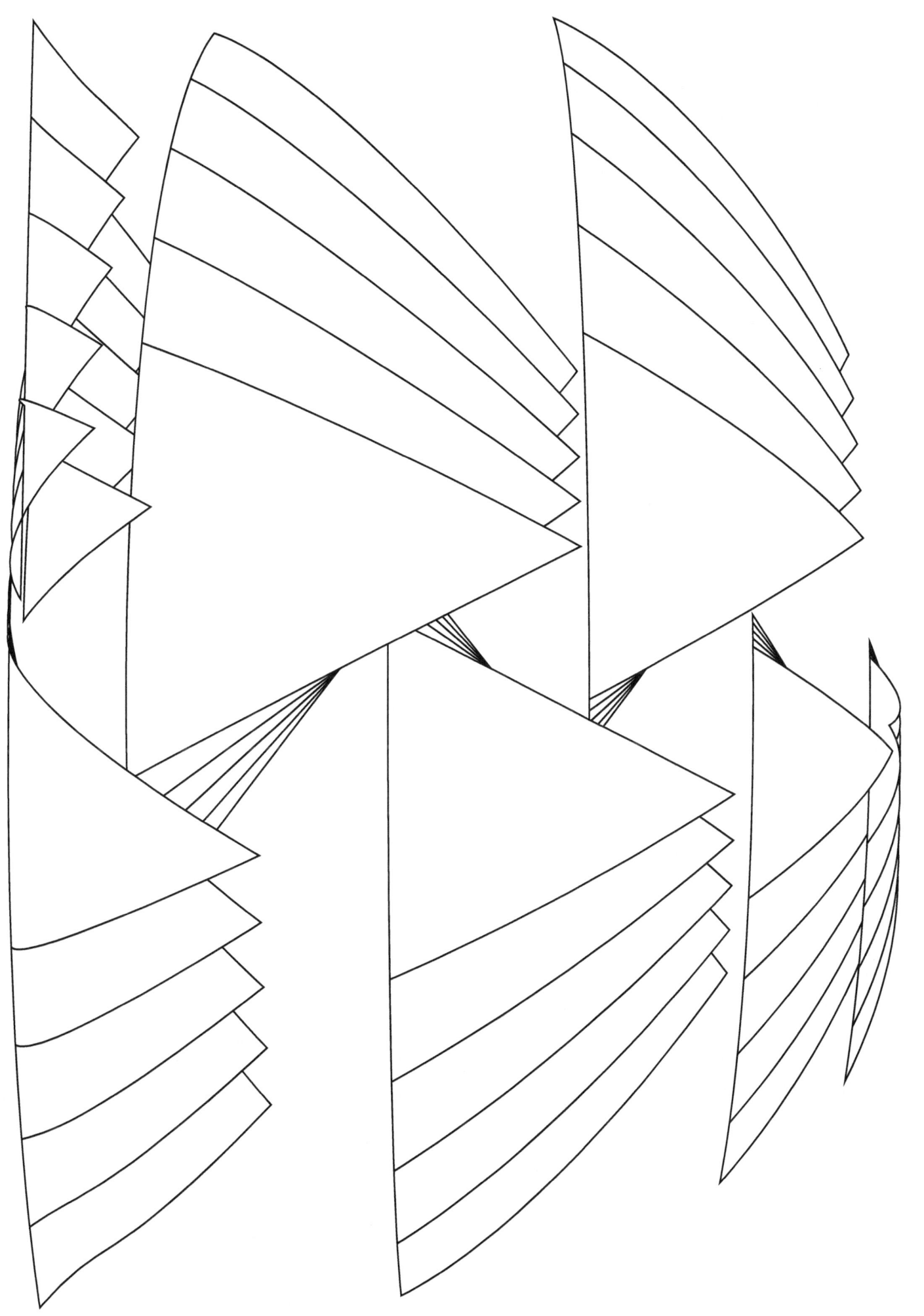

D#   46

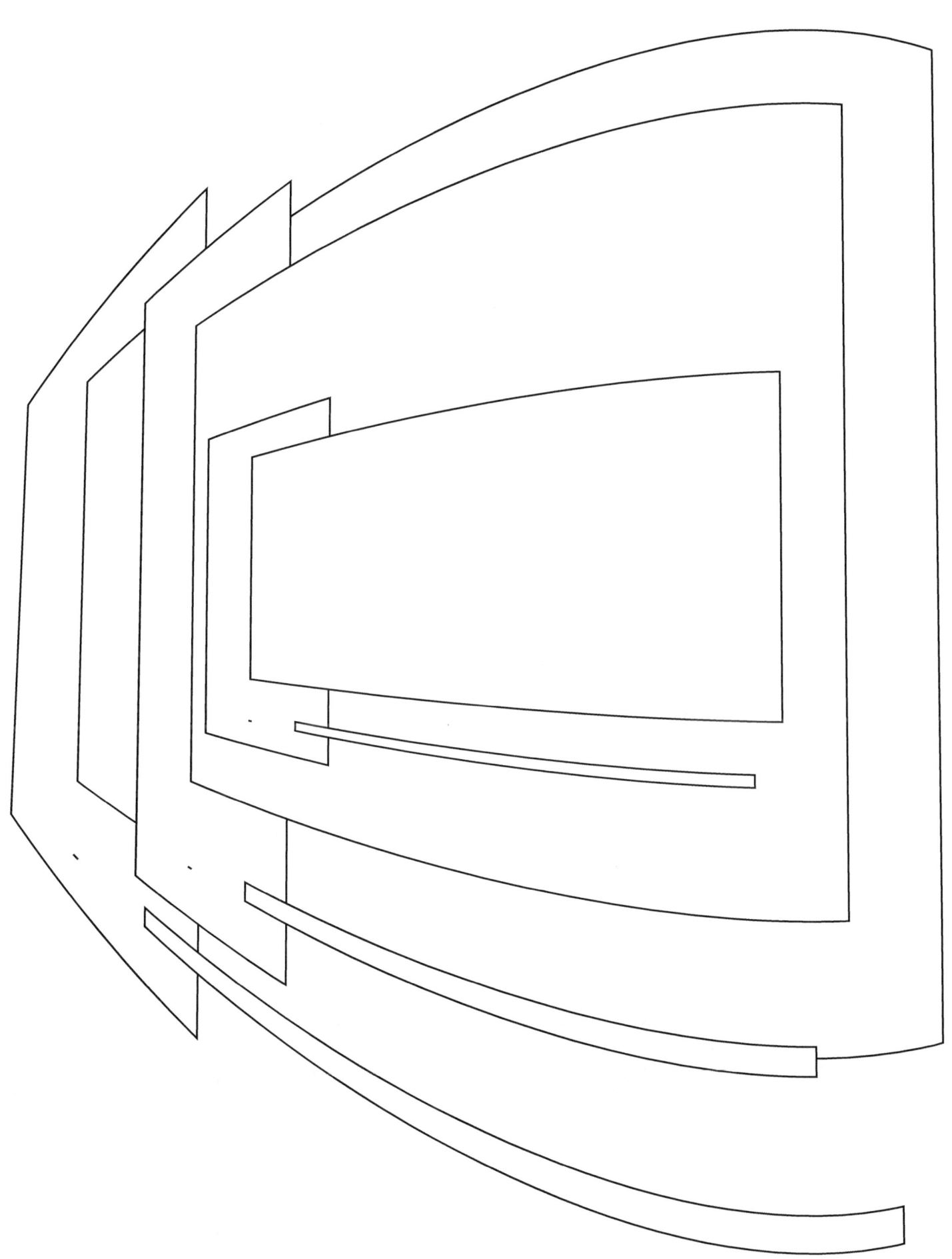

D#   50

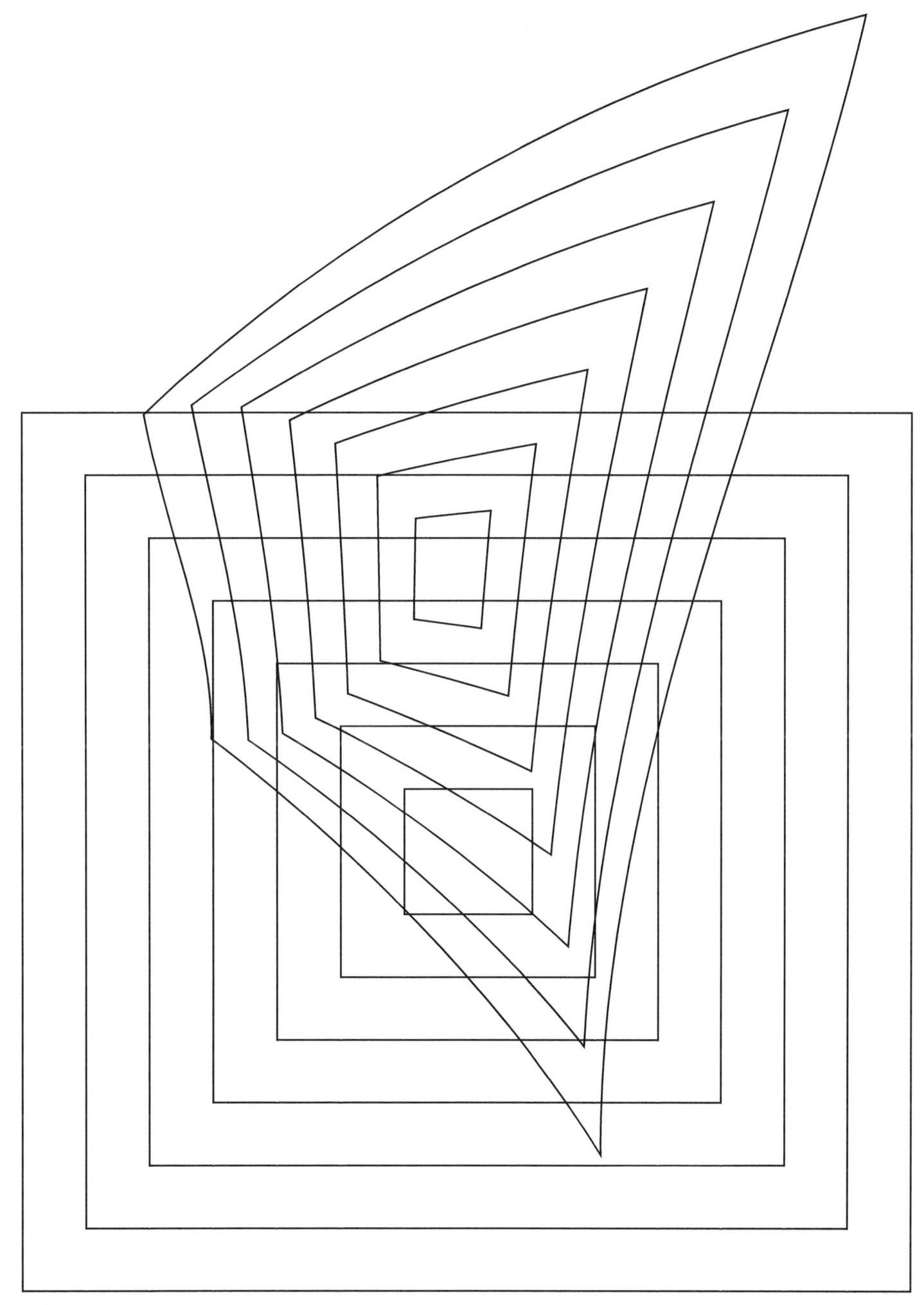

D# 32

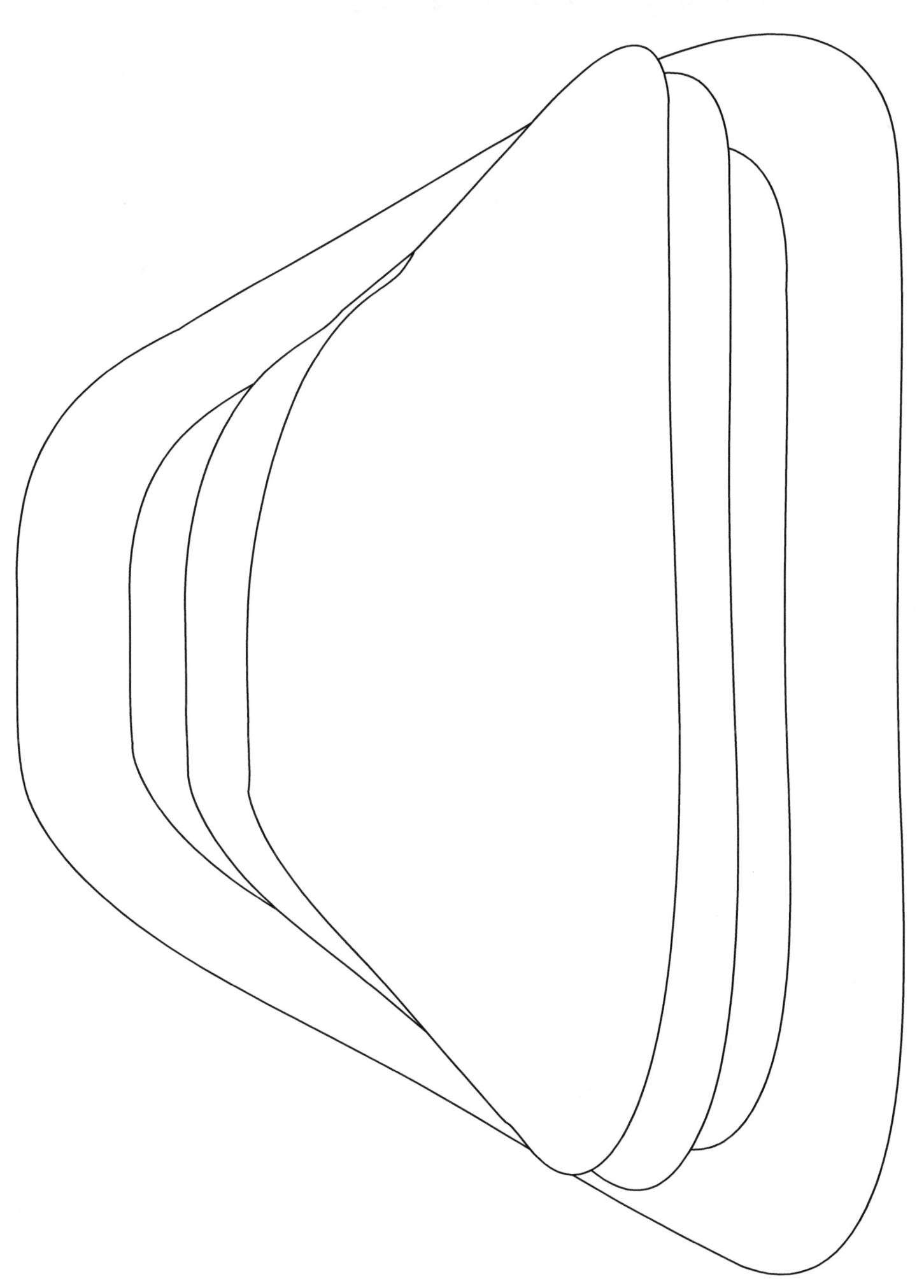

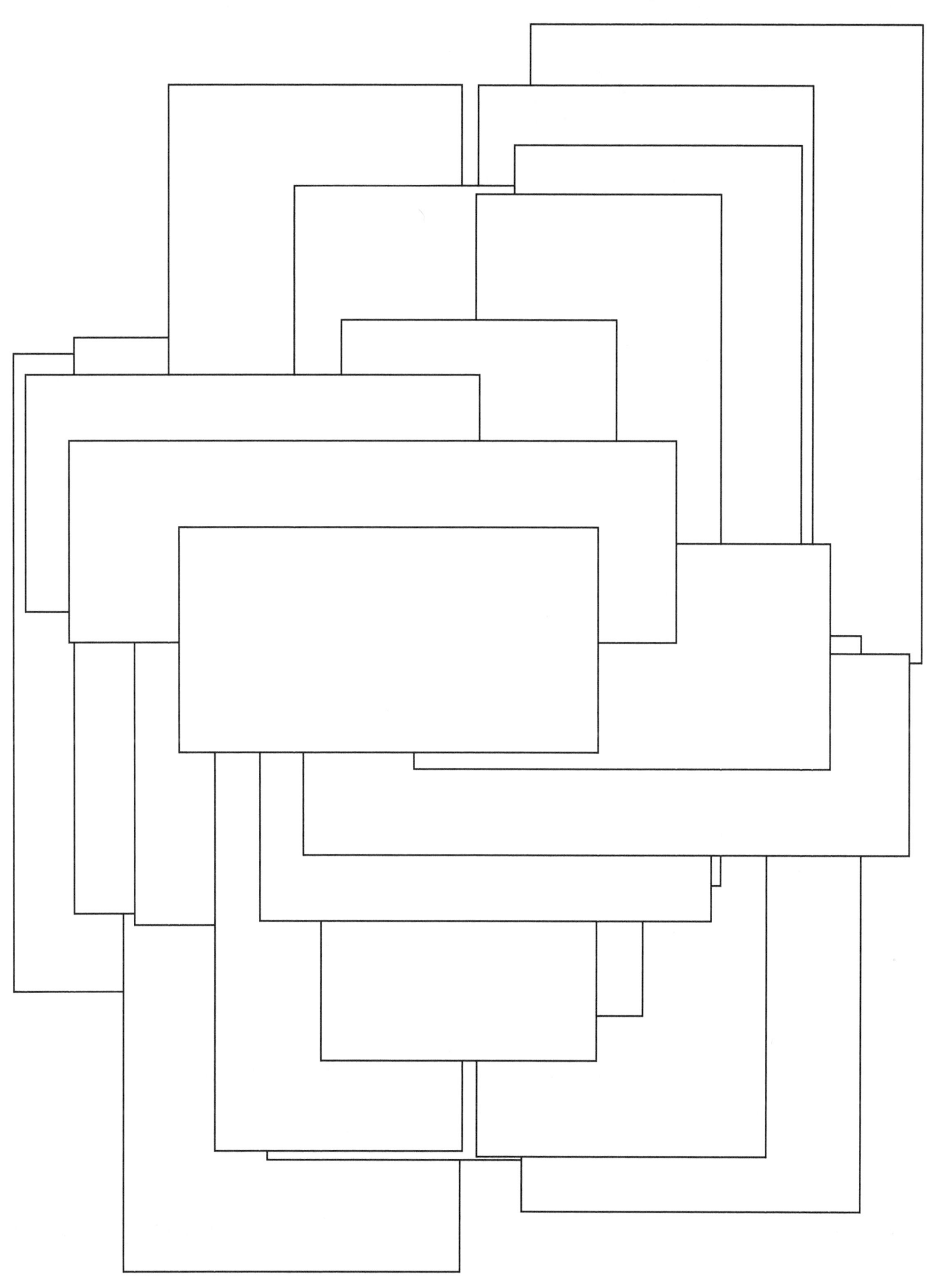

D# 39

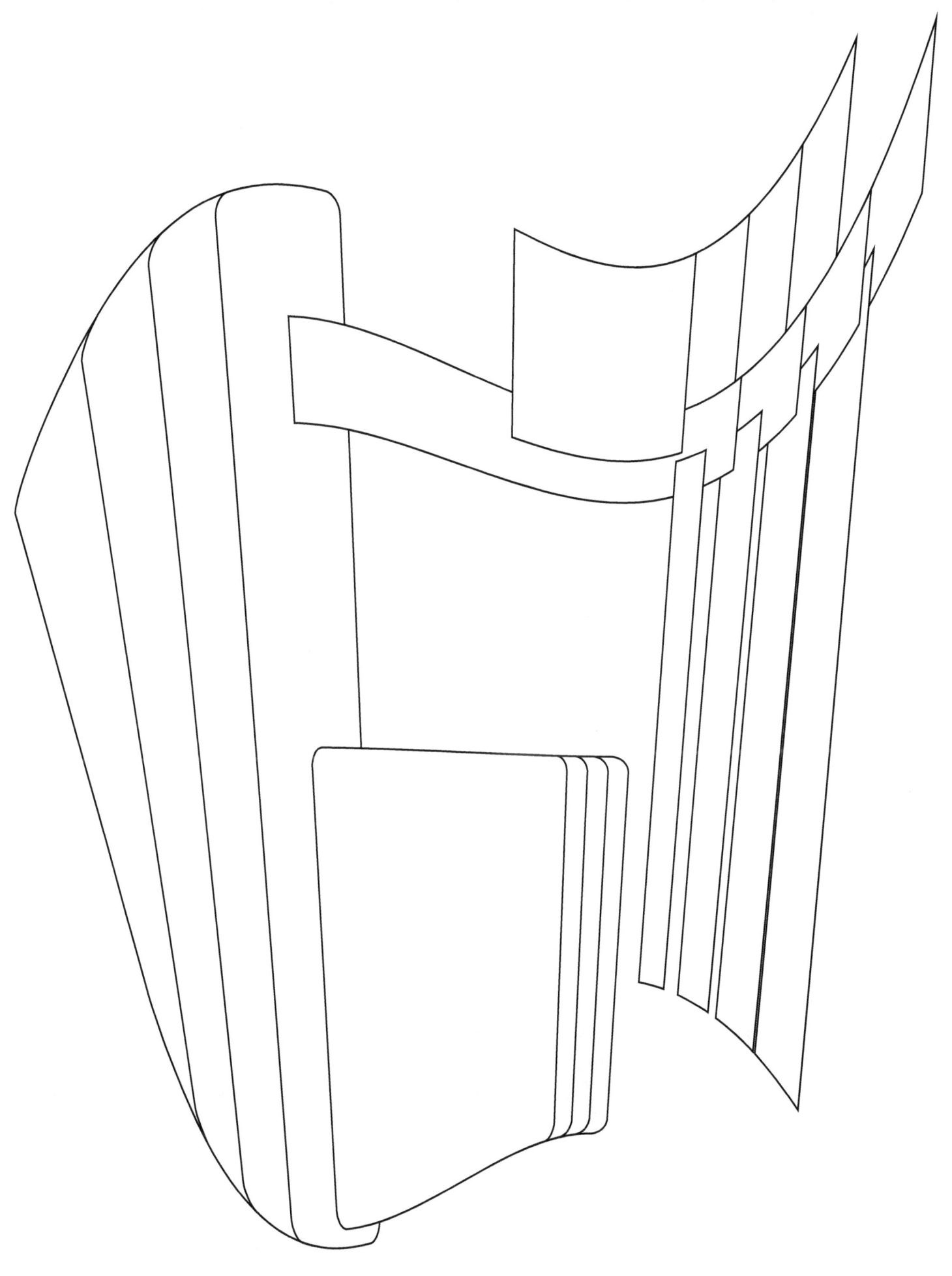

D# 61

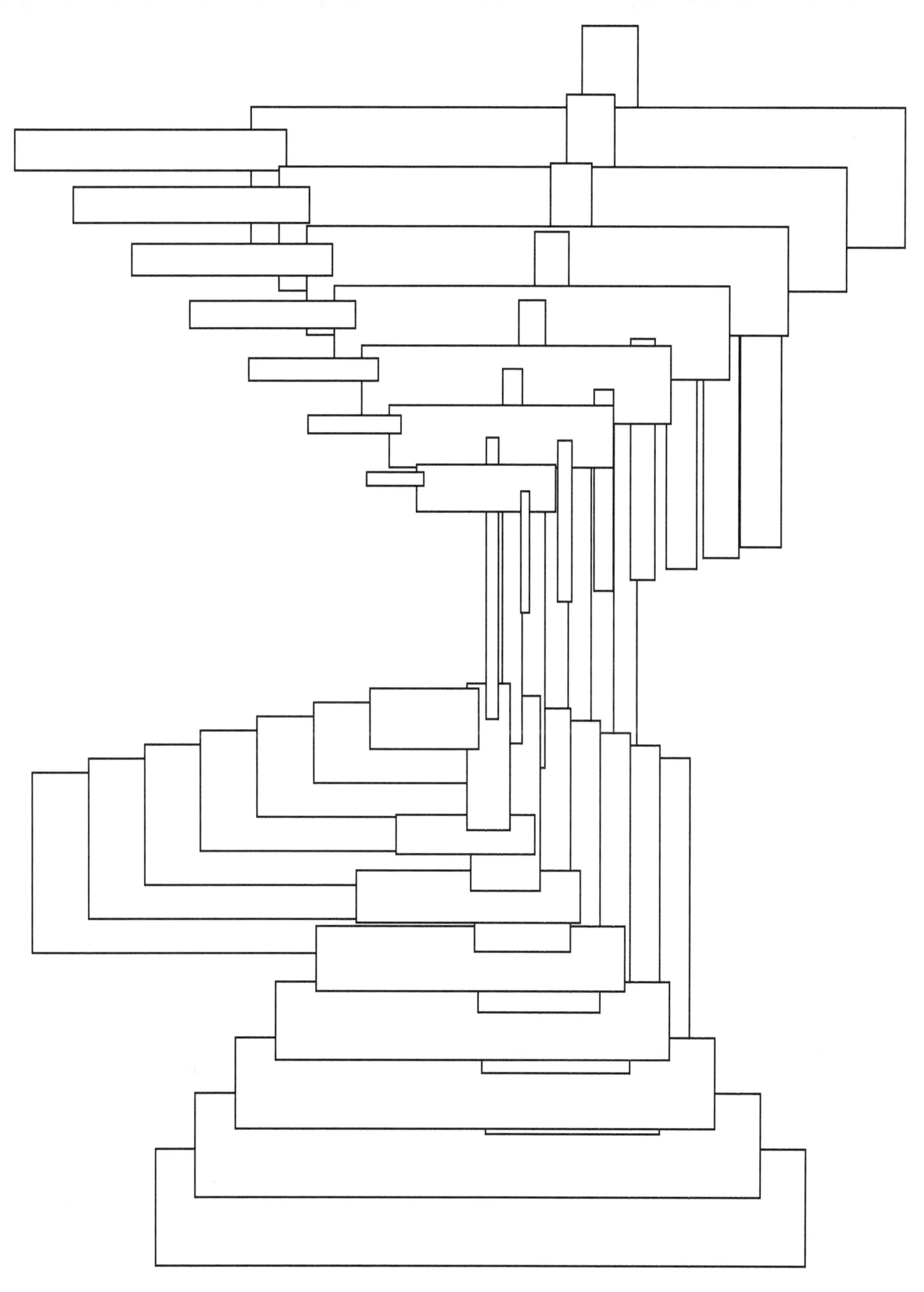

D#   43

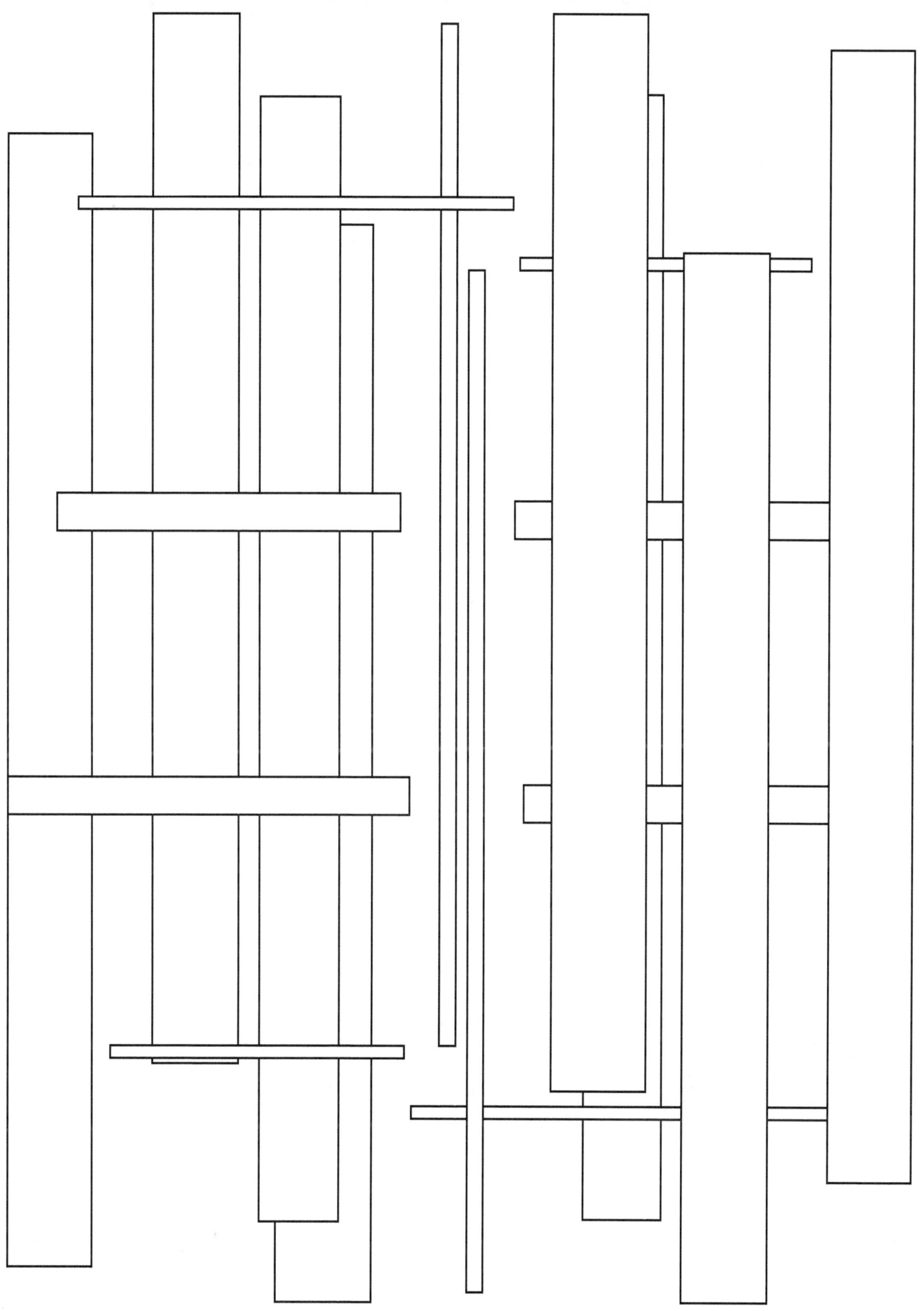

D#   44

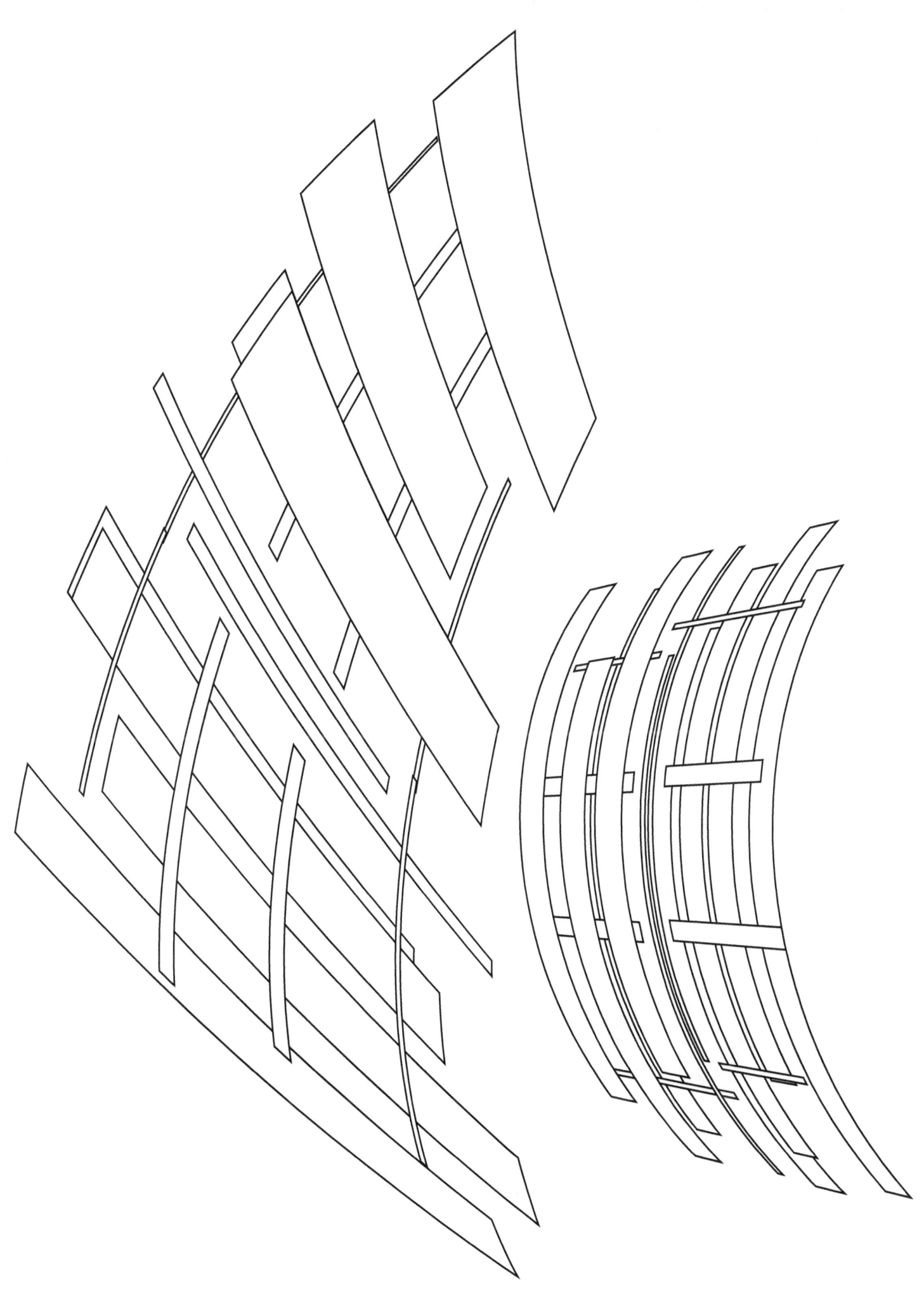

D#   42

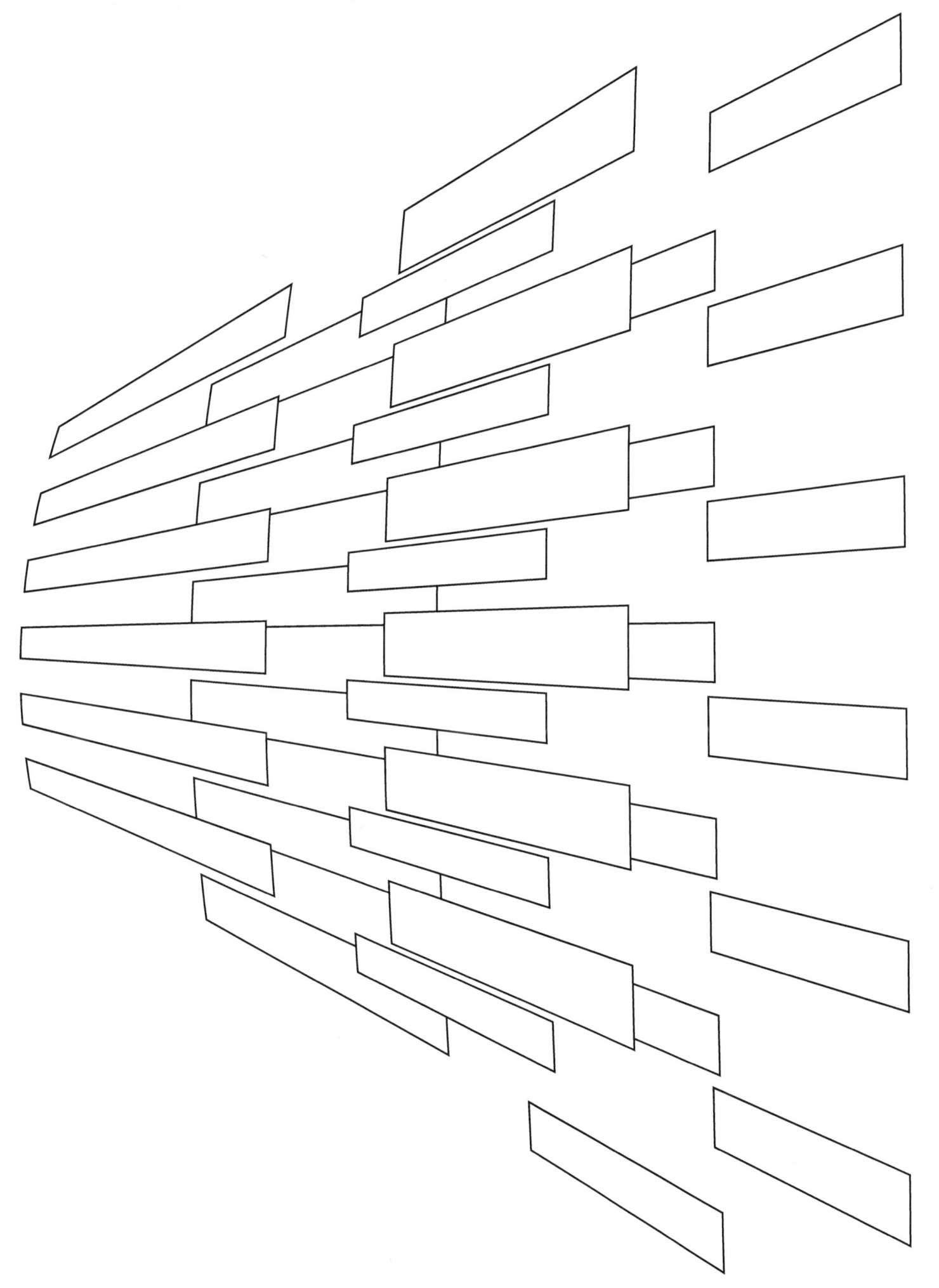

D# 48

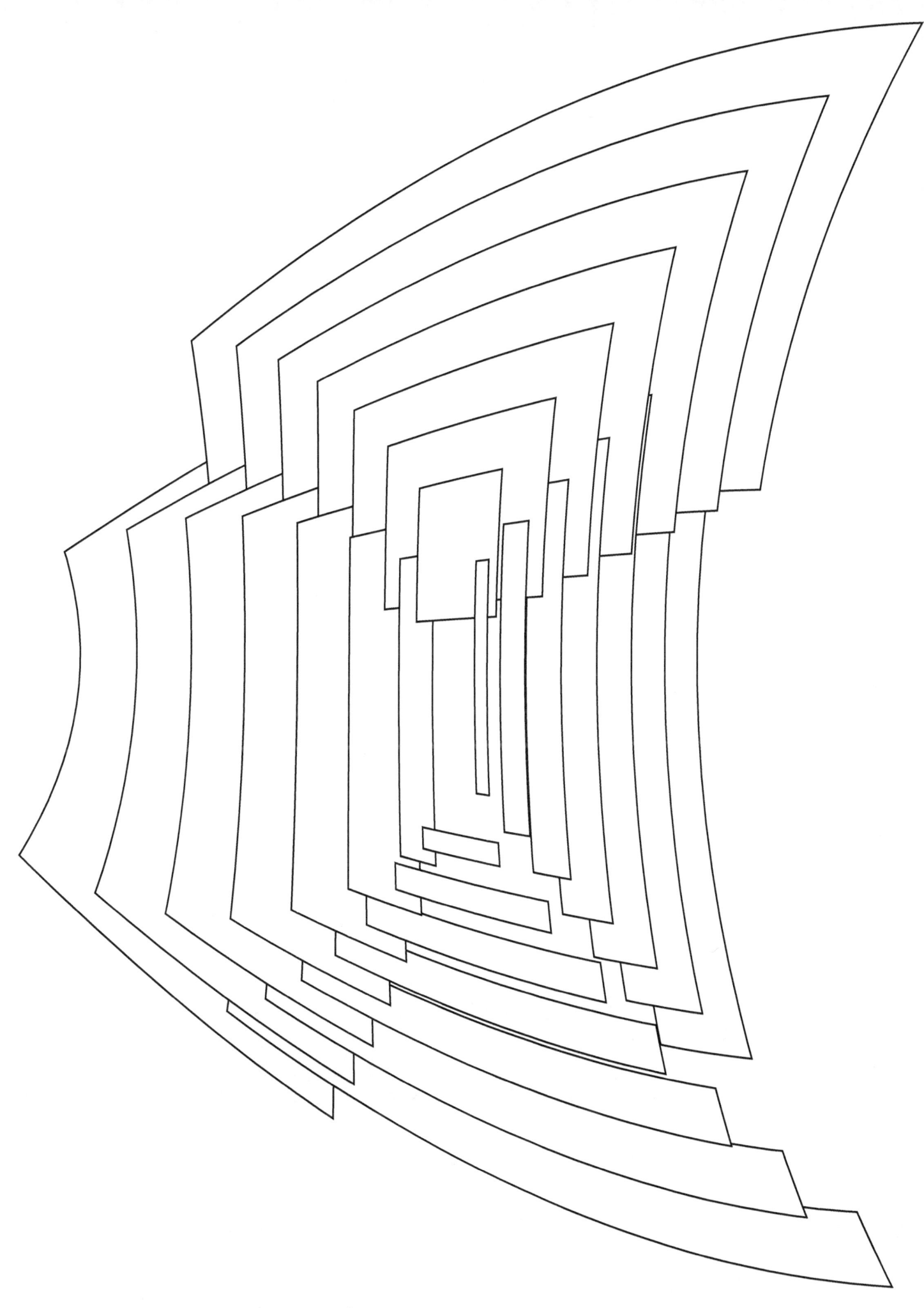

D#   76

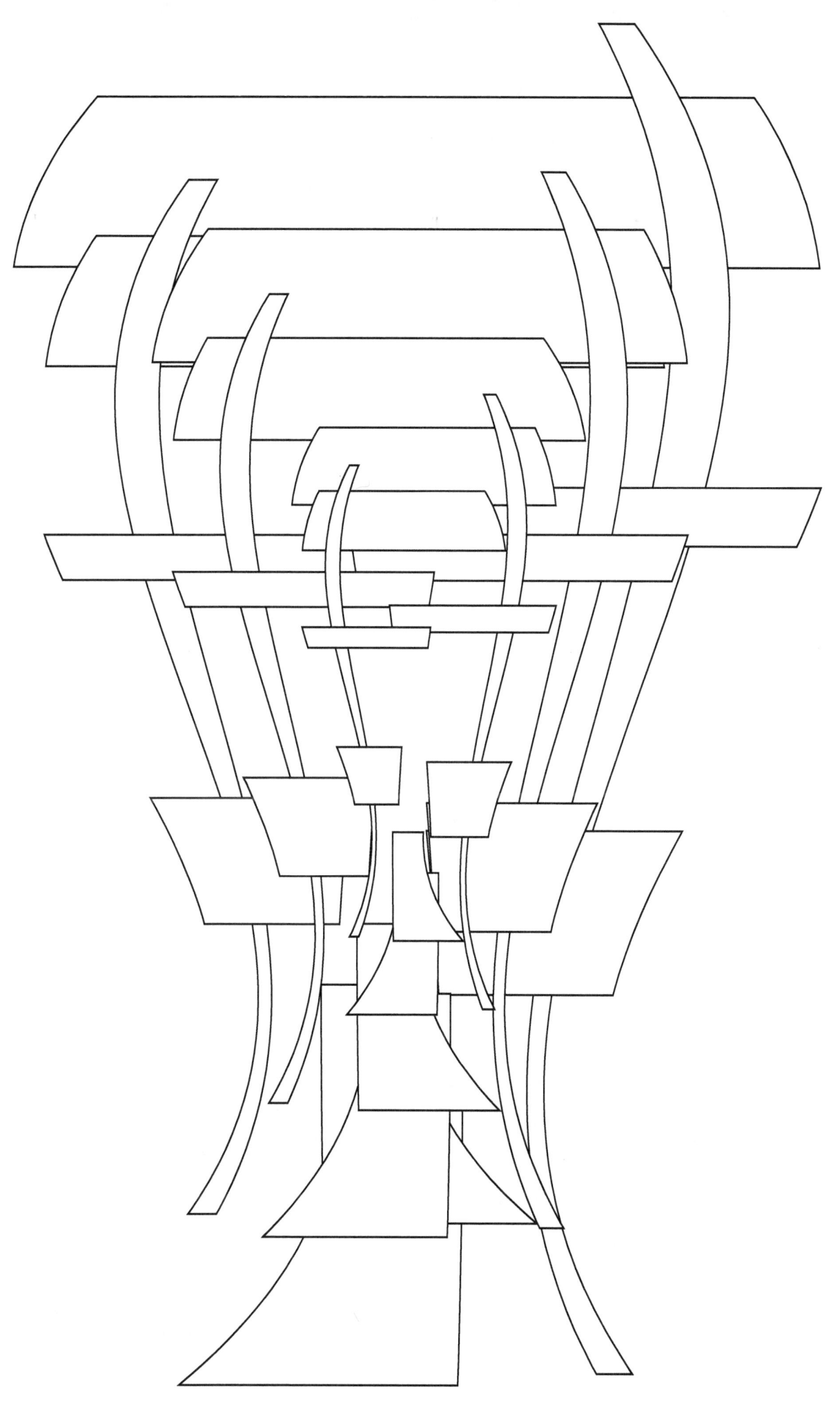

D#   73

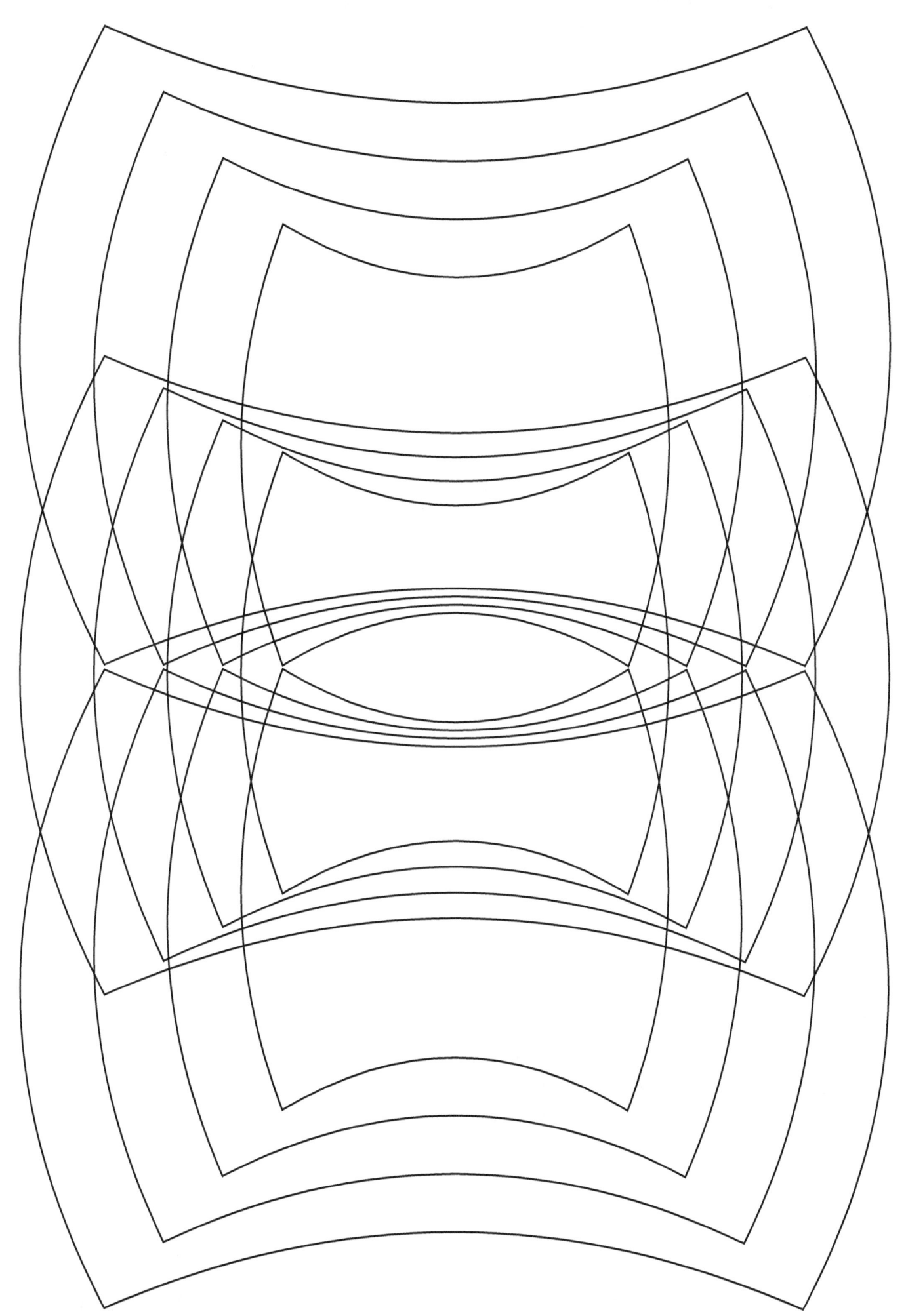

D# 52

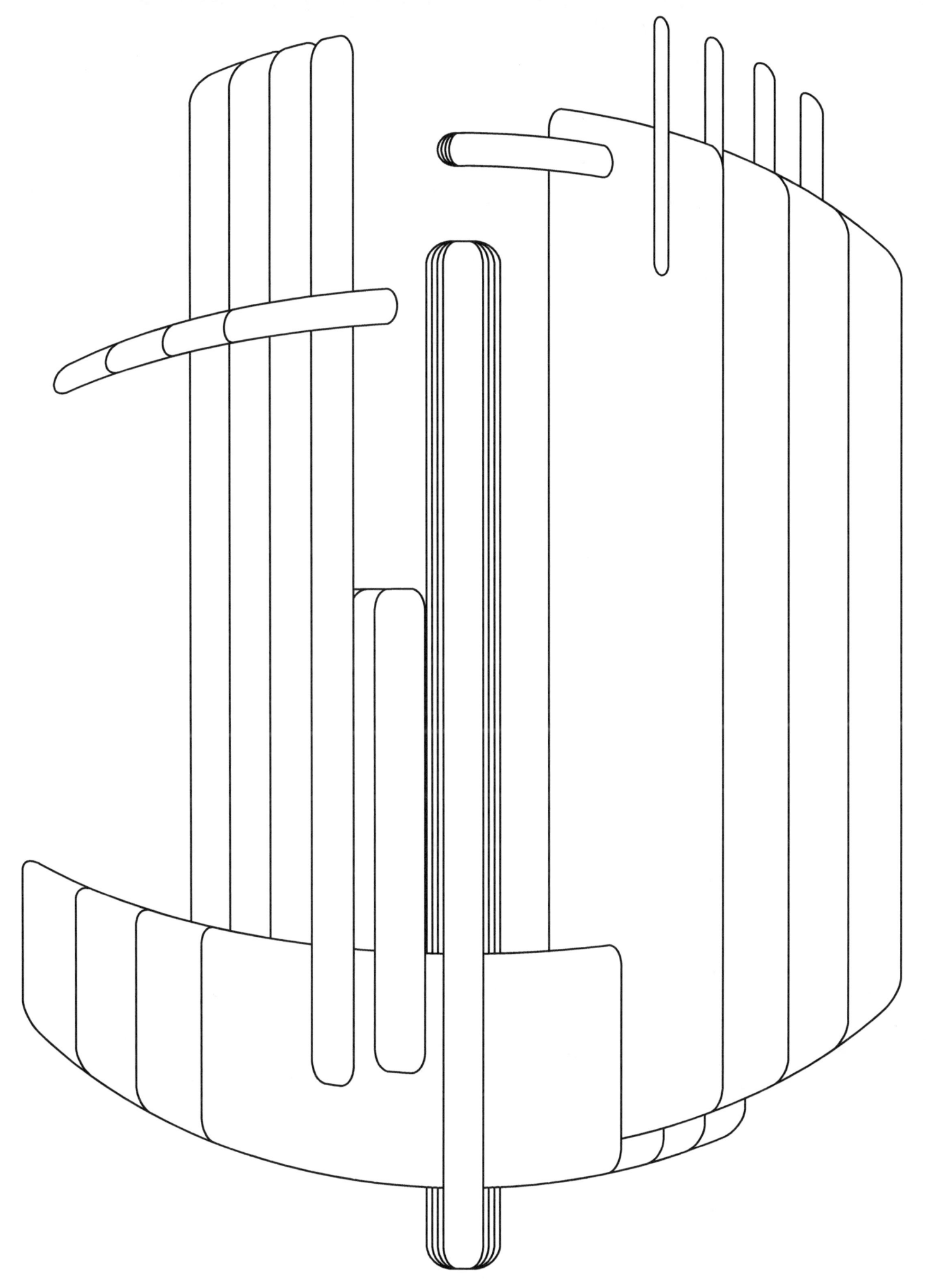

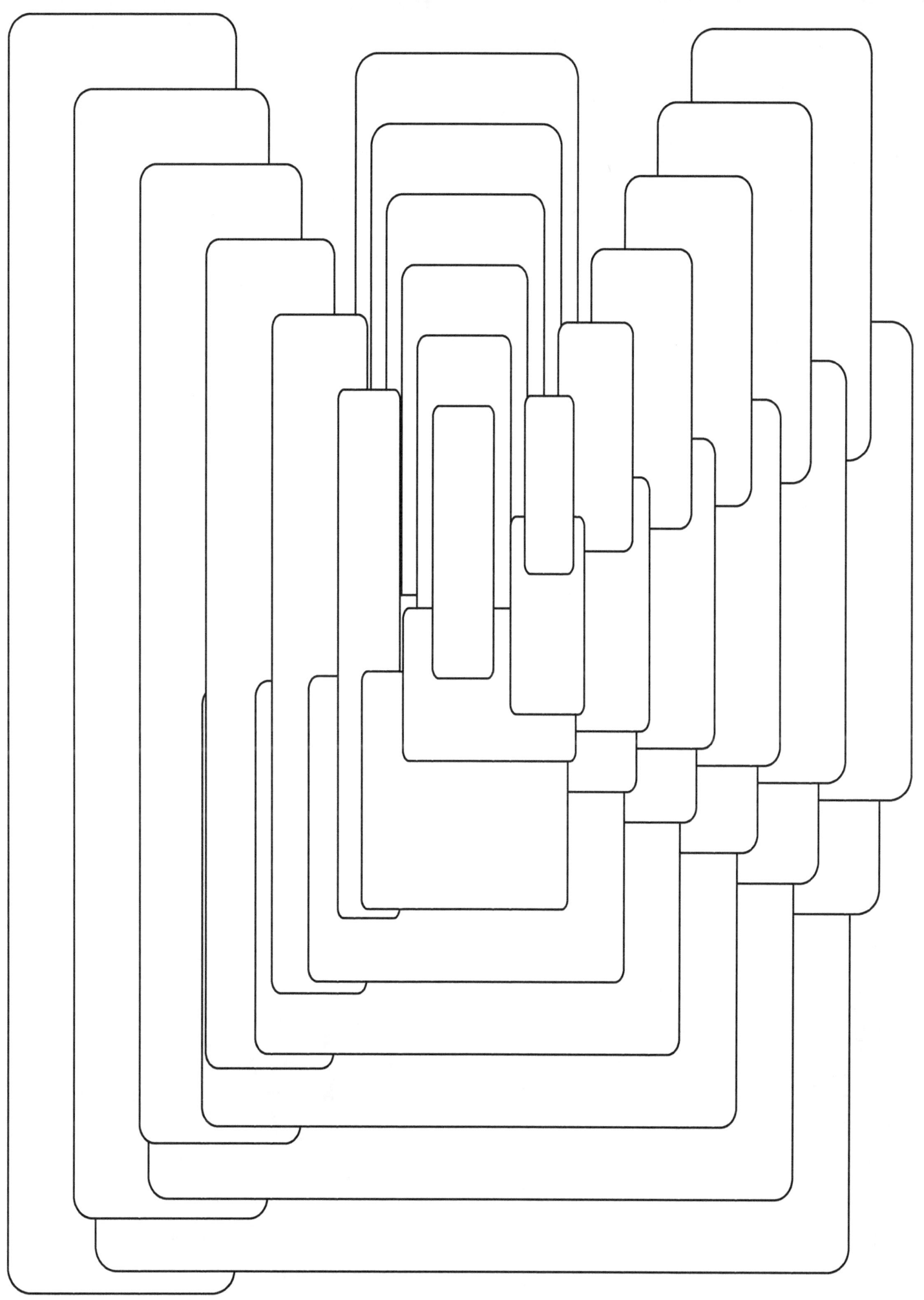

D#   55

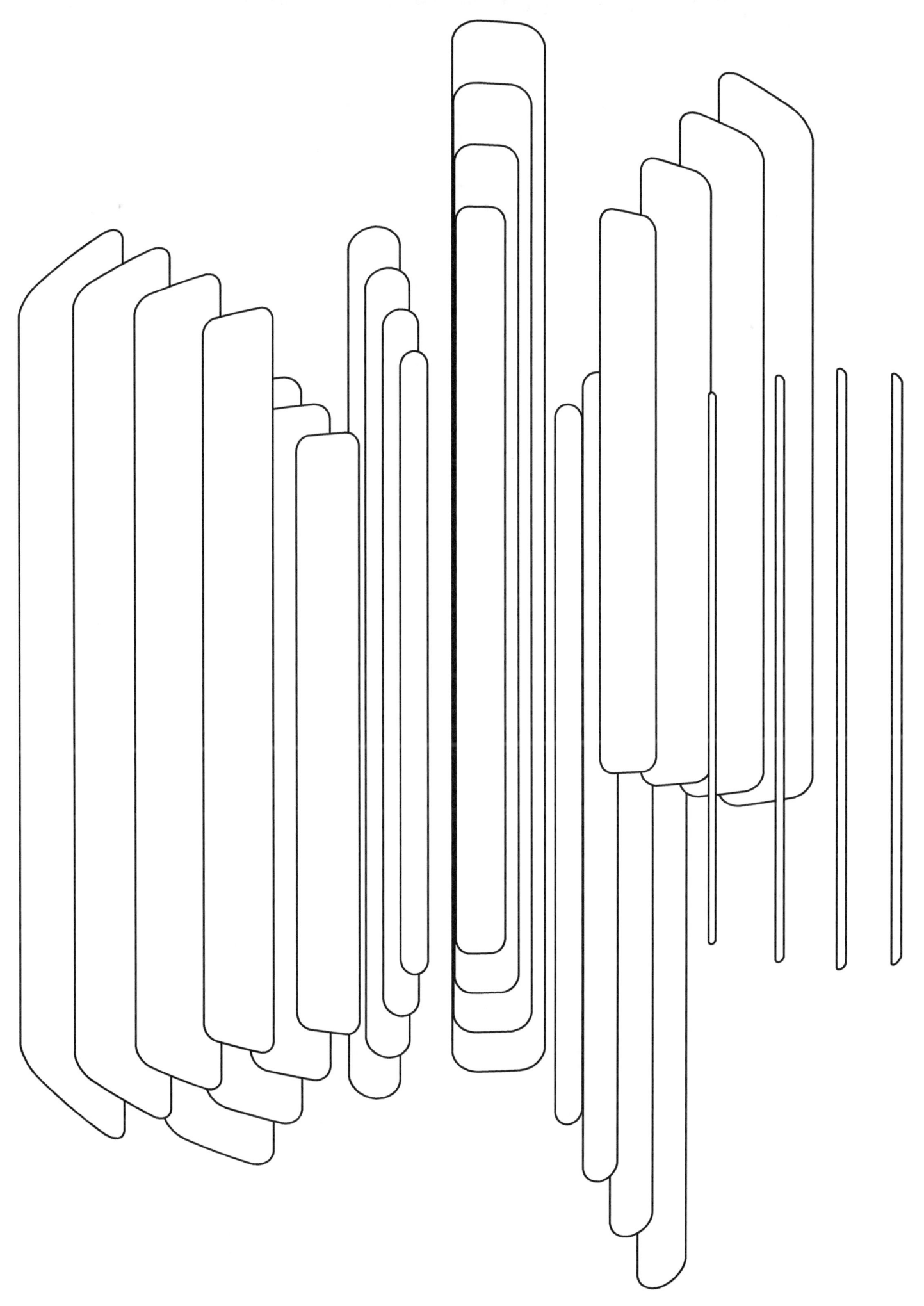

D#   56

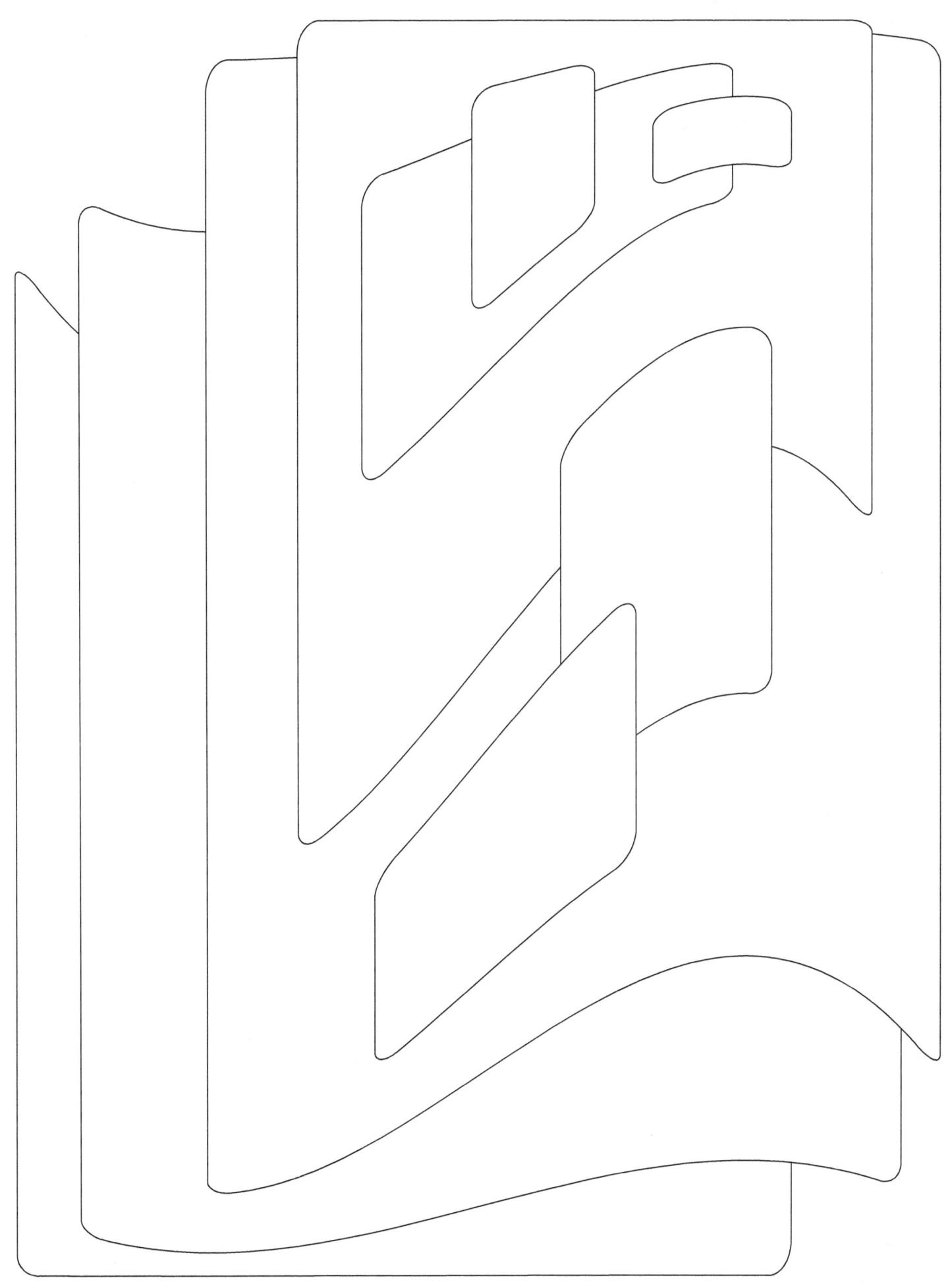

D#   59

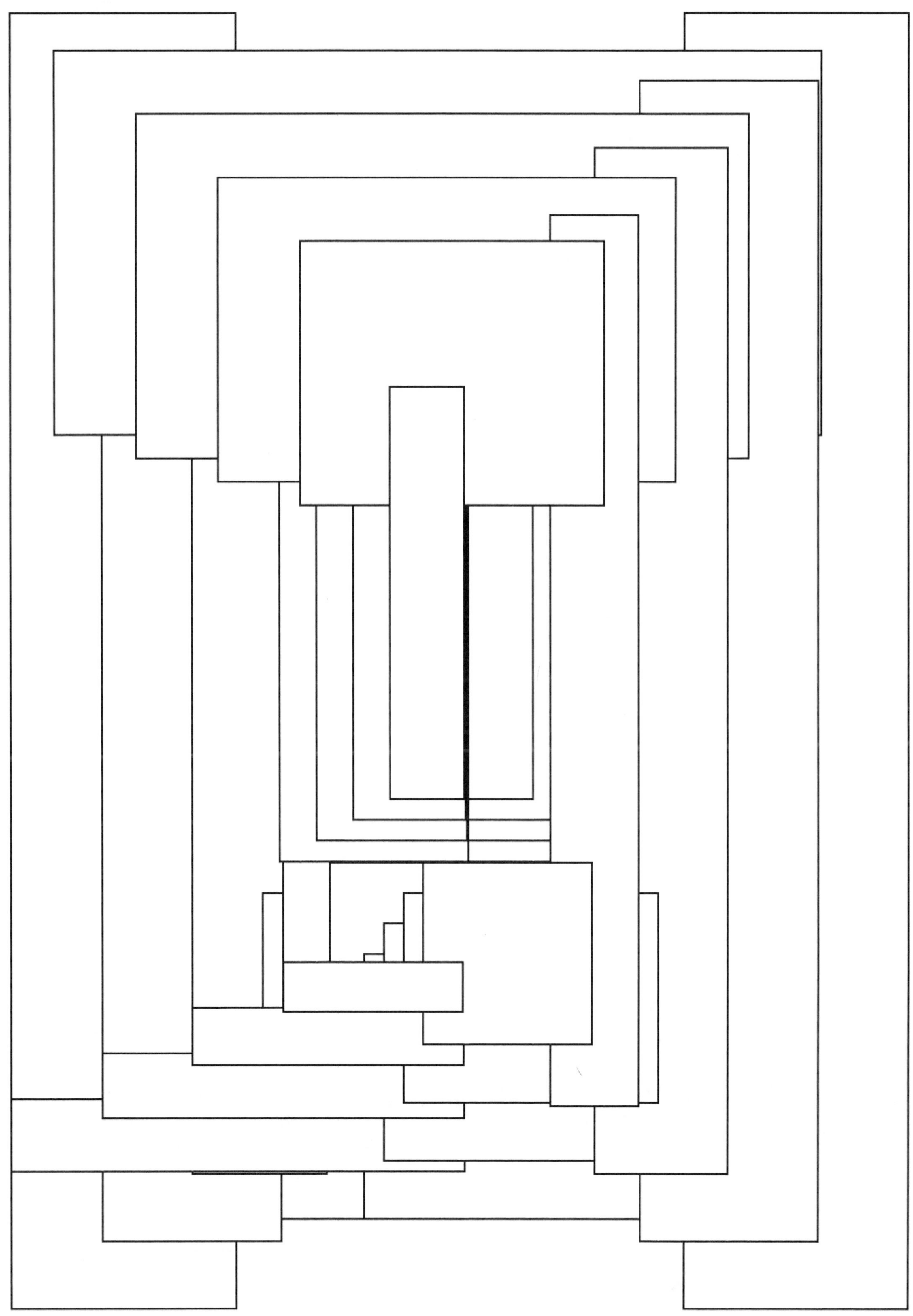

D# 58

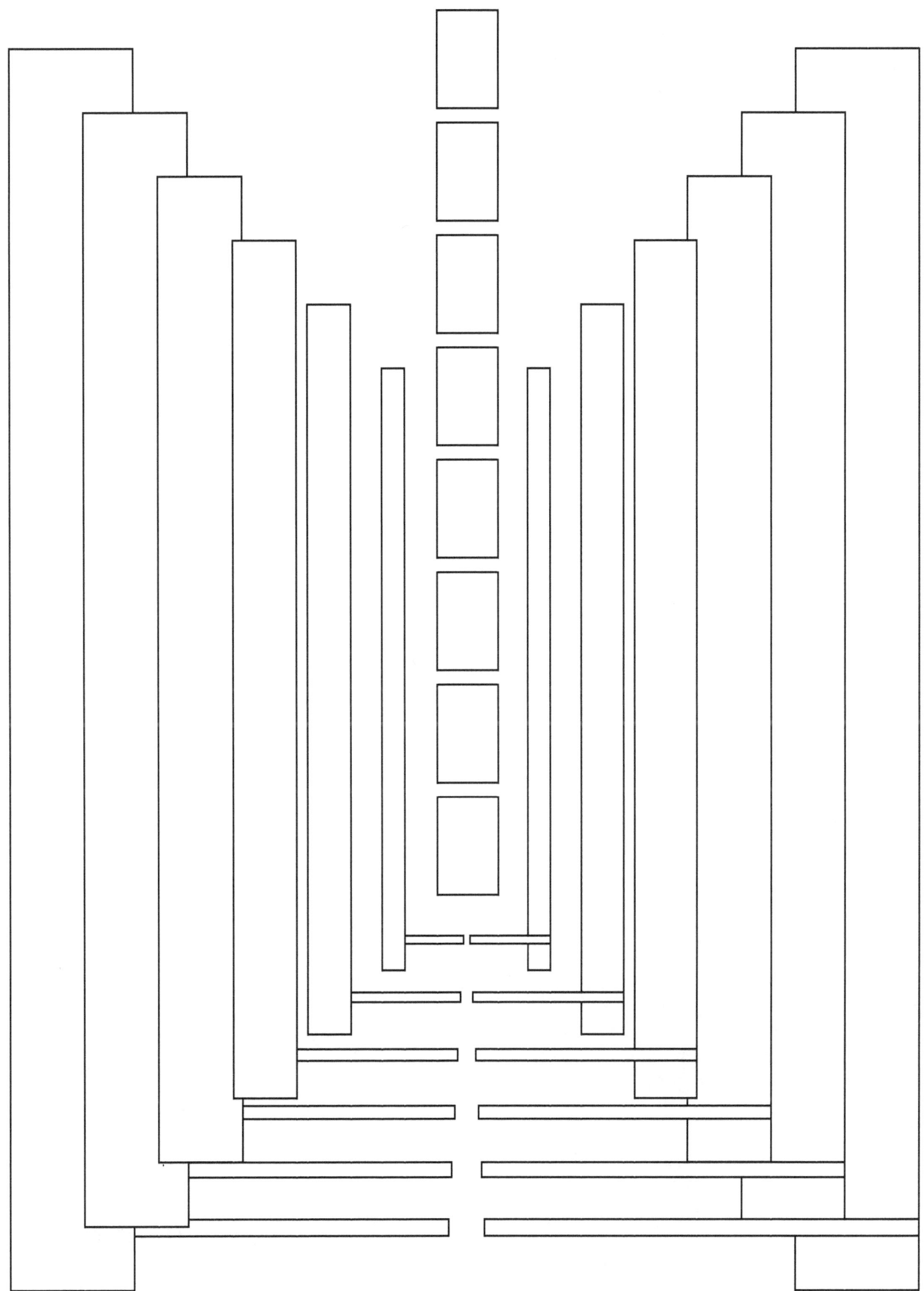

D# 60

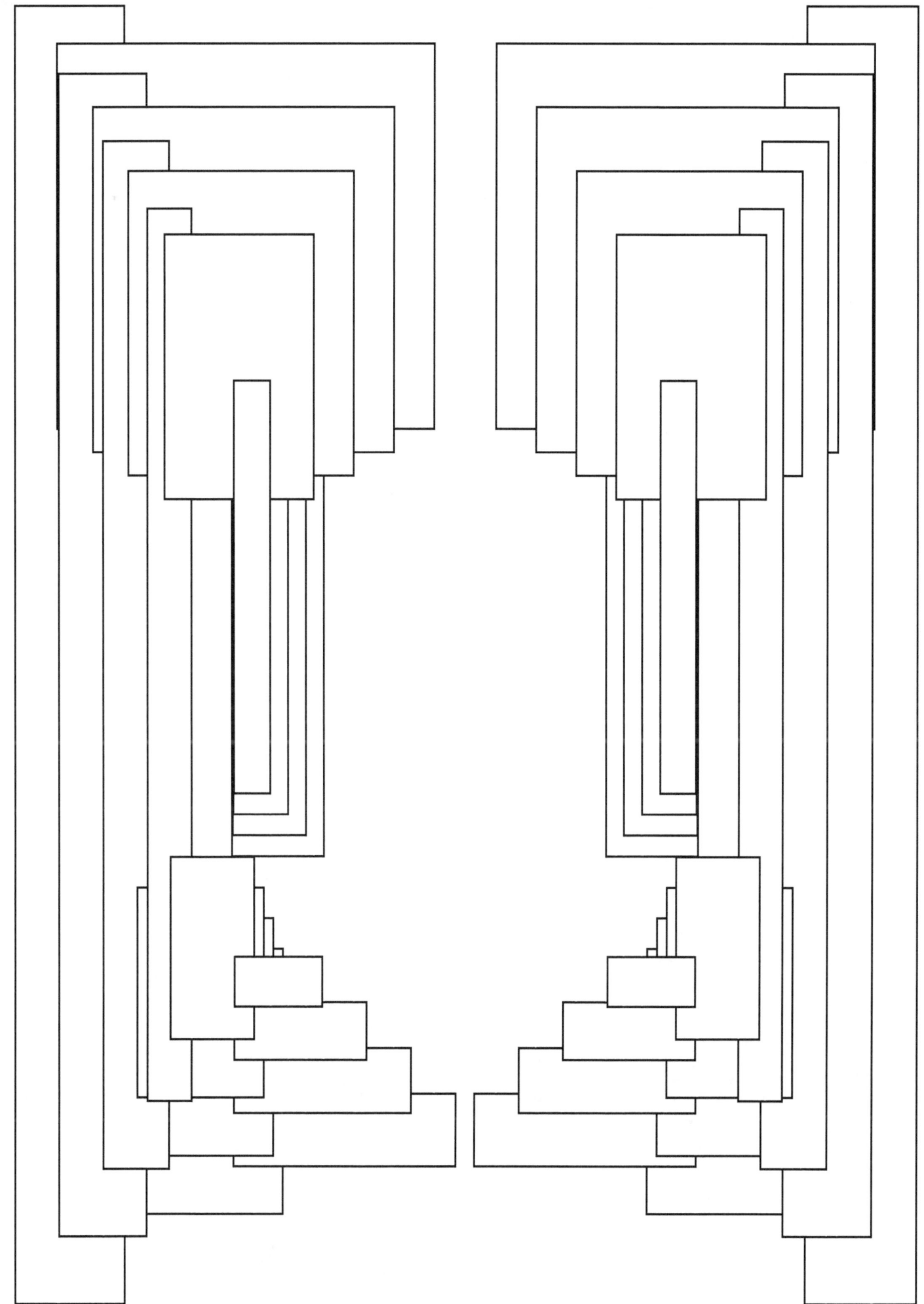

D# 64

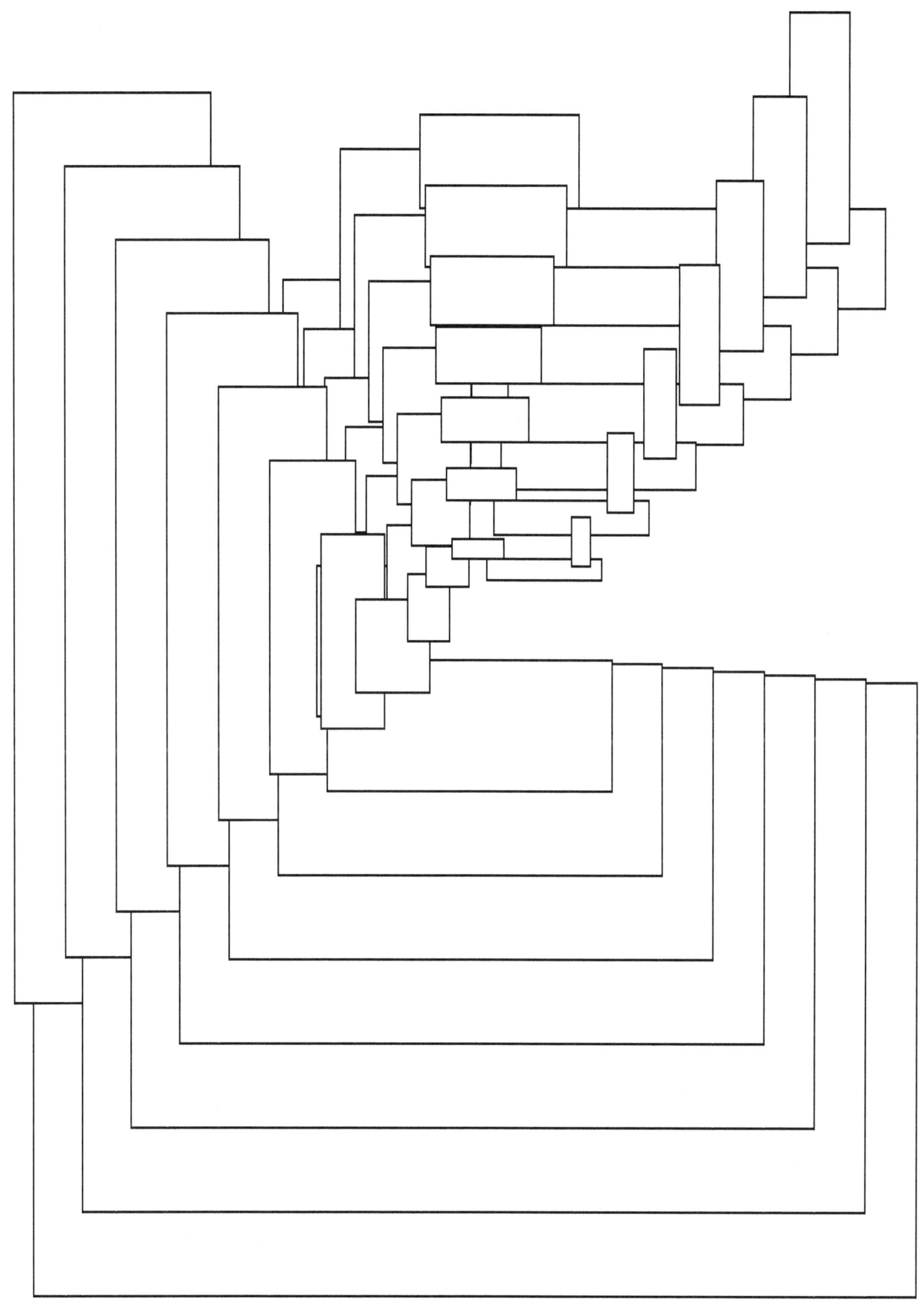

D#   54

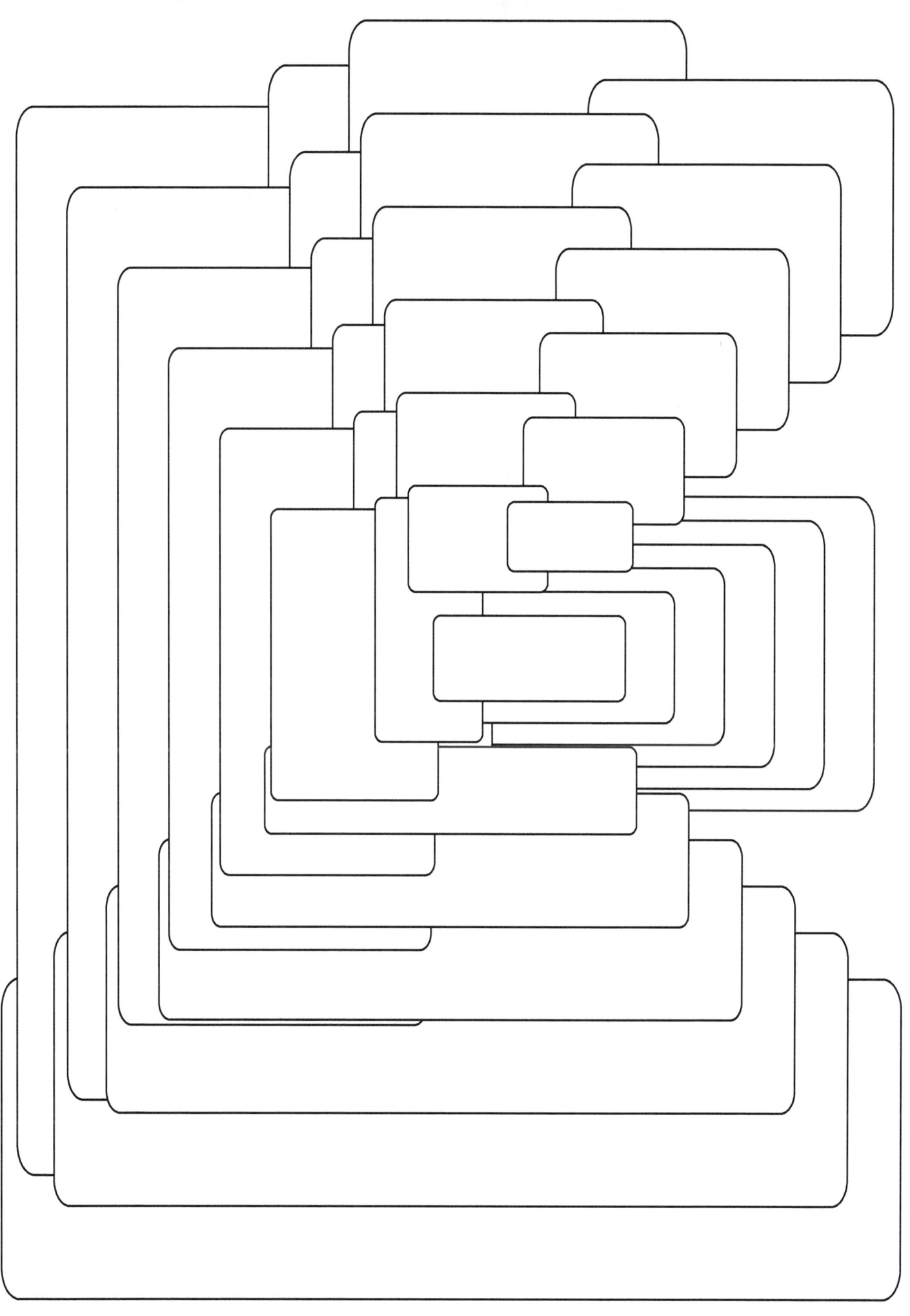